Lucrative Love

The Insider's Secrets to Marrying Millions

Tom Feltenstein

Up Your Sales Publishing
West Palm Beach, Florida

First printing 2009

ISBN 978-0-9823302-2-7

LCCN 2009924279

Up Your Sales Publishing
701 South Rosemary Avenue, Suite 313
West Palm Beach, FL 33401
561-650-1315
www.LucrativeLove.com

Table of Contents

This book can be hazardous to your current way of life. If you are content with your pathetic erxistence, working to stay afloat and where being taken to the Paddy's Dinner is reserved for special occasions; if you are happy dating from the same pool of losers and don't mind the car payments so you can have a decent ride; if you are fine with your tiny, messy apartment, then I suggest you not read this book. It will offend you. More than likely it will really piss you off. It will challenge a very core belief—*that you don't deserve better*, and that dreaming or planning for the life of your dreams is somehow shameful or sinful.

If this is the case, I suggest you close this book and give it to a friend who constantly complains about the above; a friend who would enjoy a great laugh and who might want to find millionaire to marry; a friend who is tired of living an average, ordinary life; a friend who would shoot for the stars if given the chance; a friend who wants an extraordinary life, does not mind a challenge, and is ready to have a whole lot of fun in the process.

What are the chances of you earning your way into millions? Not very high, I bet. You can fantasize about it; everybody does, but few make it. If you dare to dream of a jet-set lifestyle and you would enjoy a date with Madame Celebrity, a ring from Mr. Opulence, a weekend with Sir Fame, or a blow from Miss Flow, then you will love this book. Full of wit and humor, *Lucrative Love* pops the lid open to our silent hopes and forbidden dreams—and the harsh realities of marrying into wealth.

Tom Feltenstein

Acknowledgments

When thinking of who to acknowledge for helping to create this book, there's always the fear of leaving someone out—or worse, including one of the many who told me I was crazy and this project doomed. In truth, had it not been for those nay-sayers, I might never have dug my heels in and completed it, so I do indeed owe those detractors a note of thanks...but just a note.

One of the key factors in having an entertaining and enlightening book is the collaboration of a couple of great writers: Dee Burks and Liz Ragland. These two are cut from the same cloth as I am and added much wit and humor to the text as well as ensuring that a woman's perspective was included.

Included in the list of those who gave their all to this project and supported it are the members of my staff, including Anita Veltre, Tyler Fielding, Nancy Carver, and Natalia Creamer. My heartfelt thanks to each of you for your hard work.

There are numerous people to whom I presented the idea who voiced support and added suggestions. These include Brad Kent and Joe Lachmuth, who loved the idea and laughed right along with me as it came together into something real.

The last group I'd like to acknowledge are all the women I've loved before. It was my experiences with numerous relationships, including several marriages, which brought about the idea for this project. As you might imagine, it is my own inability to create and preserve my own relationships that started my mind pondering on other ways to being about something lasting.

Since writing this book, I've been asked if I believe in love. The answer is absolutely yes. I've wanted it and sought it all my life just as many of you have, and I'm still looking. We are imperfect people in an insane world and love is the only thing that makes any part of it worth living. While the ideas and thoughts in this book are fun and interesting to contemplate, the most important idea to take away is that if you seek what you desire you will attain it—and if that is love you will find it.

About the Author

A GENUINE ST. JOSEPHS, MISSOURI, born blueblood, Tom Feltenstein spent his teen years hobnobbing with the who's who from East Coast aristocracy. He is a world recognized marketing strategist, speaker, and consultant to top corporations and Fortune 500 companies, plus thousands of small businesses. He has been featured on CNN's *Larry King Live, The David Letterman Show,* and the Fox News *Pre-Game Show,* and in *USA Today, Wall Street Journal,* and countless others for his marketing acumen and witty dose of Uncommon Wisdom.

Tom became a millionaire after his first marriage (prior to this, he was a multimillionaire). A business strategist par excellence in *Lucrative Love,* Tom takes you step-by-step and delineates the actions and tactics you need to take to find and marry your diamond.

Tom has two wonderful grown children and lives in Palm Beach, Florida. He is single and looking for a gorgeous, outgoing, kind, witty, affectionate, independent woman (39 to 50) who loves to travel and has a healthy sexual appetite—and big boobs.

One: Cinderella Lied

I've never lived in a building without my name on it.
—Ivanka Trump

WE'VE ALL HEARD THE STORY OF CINDERELLA. The poor girl was forced to scour the floor on her hands and knees, do the laundry, and cater to every whim of her wicked stepmother and stepsisters. As she watched the gruesome twosome prepare for the ball, she silently wished she could go as well. Sadly, she had to stay home and scrub her sisters' whiskers out of the wash basin while they shamelessly squeezed their boobs together so the prince could catch a glimpse of their cleavage. And so the story goes—her animals come to life, an old bag lady conjures up a pumpkin, dolls her up, sends her to the ball, she meets the prince, and they get married and live happily ever after while her stepsisters sit at home and grow old and lonely. Sweet isn't it?

I can't help but wonder, though, if Cinderella married the prince because she actually loved him or if it had more to do with his castle and fortune. We are raised with the idea that our wedding day is supposed to be one of the most meaningful, important days of our lives. Candles, flowers, cake, white dress (for some anyway), and little birdies tweeting in a nearby tree. Church pews jam-packed with family and friends all there to witness the blessed event.

What none of them realizes is that baby girl is marrying a trash collector whose annual salary is less than her daddy's country club membership. But it's all going to be okay because they love each other. Love will carry them through the good

1

and bad times, right? Wrong! More likely, sooner rather than later, baby girl's going to get tired of Prince Charming coming home smelling like dirty diapers and rancid grease.

And don't think this scenario happens to women only. Men are faced with the same situations too. Remember the fairy tale story about kissing a frog to get a prince? That's because some poor guy got himself saddled with a trophy wife, and yeah, she looks hot and all, but she has to close her eyes and imagine someone else to let him get within ten feet of her. Refilling that Viagra prescription every month can take its toll as well. Aside from the fabulous roll in the hay, what does he really have in common with her other than a bank account? (Oh, and just a word of caution guys: If your needle is standing in the haystack for more than eight hours, you might want to call a doctor.)

Let's take a moment and travel back in time to the weddings of several hundred years ago. On occasion, a farm boy would fall in love with the milk maid's jugs, and they'd tie the knot. For the most part, however, marriages were arranged. The participants in these marriages had very little, if any, choice of who their spouse might be. Interestingly enough, the men had just as little say in this matter as the women of the time.

Marriages were frequently arranged so both families involved would benefit. They were arranged to bring prestige, wealth, or political power to the family. The children of landowners would be expected to marry children of other landowners to increase the size of the acreage.

One of the most famous examples of the tradition of arranged marriage was between King Henry VIII and his fourth wife Anne of Cleves. After he whacked the heads off his previous brides, he got tired of whacking something else off, so he decided to find a young lady to give him a hand. He was sent a royal portrait of a beautiful young princess. Henry immediately sent for her, and when she arrived they were married. A very short time afterward, Henry woke up one morning and realized she wasn't as attractive as he'd hoped. So he divorced her.

But don't feel too sorry for poor old Henry. Many a young lass around the castle were more than willing to let His Highness the Porker pork her to get some of the fringe benefits of bedding a royal. And don't pretend to be shocked. I know women who will give it up for a ride in a Mercedes and dinner at the country club. So who's the "ho"? Is it any wonder prostitution is the oldest profession? You give me this, I'll give you that; a simple transaction.

Of course, back in ye olden times, many of these couples didn't even meet until their wedding day. I can't imagine schlepping down the aisle to spend the rest of my life with someone only to find him or her toothless and covered with boils. In his *Utopia*, Sir Thomas More recommended that, in order to avoid subsequent disappointments such as a teeny peenie or boobs that resemble a potato in a tube sock, couples should see one another's bodies before marriage.

One morning, Sir William Roper visited More in Chelsea to request marriage to one of his daughters. Roper was ushered into the girls' room where they were sleeping on their backs. Without a word, More ripped the sheets from the bed. The girls awoke with a shock, and as soon as they saw Roper standing over them, they quickly rolled on to their stomachs. "Now I have seen both sides," Roper remarked, and chose the elder daughter, Margaret, to be his wife. Maybe this is where the phrase "shoot for the moon" came from. It may also be where a woman's desire for bigger and better ta-tas started. I bet the younger sister stewed over that one for years!

All of this sounds a bit extreme, and I'm the first to admit that I personally wouldn't want to be a part of an arranged marriage, but I must tell you what I really like about this concept. Somebody made this decision using their right judgment with a cool head, thinking about all factors for the future wellbeing of the entire family. The decision was not made by an irrationally emotional male with a hormone-infested bloodstream asking his sweetheart to tie the knot as a lame attempt to immortalize the momentary sex-based high.

My mother always told me, "You can't base your marriage on love alone," and the older I get the more I agree with her. The Romans had an interesting view toward marriage: *matrimonia debent esse libera,* or "marriages ought to be free." This meant that either spouse could opt out of the marriage if things weren't working; it was the original no-fault divorce.

There is a second benefit to arranged marriages. Your choice of finding the right partner has been eliminated, all the emphasis is on you to *be* the right partner—to work on yourself and become a better human being to relate better to your spouse. This is, perhaps, a lesson we should all remember.

Life will throw plenty of crap your way, especially when you are one-half of a couple. Love alone can't cut it, won't cut it, has no chance of ever cutting it. Life and marriage, no matter how lofty the hormone high, must be designed and lived with real common sense. By the way, in this day, "common sense" is measured in dollars and cents. And be forewarned: Common sense doesn't always feel or sound good. Often it really sucks. But life does not care if it sounds good, or if you like it. The mature soul understands that life is impersonal and has rules. Follow them and prosper, or violate them and suffer.

Money is a huge part of marriage, make no mistake. Ignore the principle and you are on the road to another divorce statistic. Follow the rule and prosper. Master the rule, and you can have anything you want.

Victorian England had a vastly different view. Society frowned on divorce, and those who did divorce would likely

> Life and marriage, no matter how lofty the hormone high, must be designed and lived with real common sense.

find themselves as social outcasts. In those days, when you got married, you stayed married regardless of situation or circumstance. No matter how many times King Henry smacked you around with a turkey leg, your only option was to find a bowl of gravy—or get beheaded.

In the present century, this view may still prevail, depending on where you live. Uptight busybodies and moral crusaders are having a field day predicting, like always, dire consequences for the "social fabric" if the institution of marriage is changed. Obviously these people have never sat in front of a stack of bills two miles high contemplating killing your spouse because of his or her credit card debt. I find it interesting that even the dowagers refer to marriage as an institution, which is where you will end up if you don't plan ahead and treat your marriage as a business.

Of course, the other reason for this Pollyanna viewpoint is that they themselves are stuck in a bad marriage and want the rest of the world to suffer with them. If I could buy stock in a vibrator company these days, I would because every morally upstanding woman has a drawer full of them.

There are many different and complex causes and reasons for divorce: infidelity, incompatibility, and growing apart, to name a few. But the main reason for the skyrocketing divorce rate today is financial problems. Yeah, this is the kind of common sense no one wants to talk about, and few have the stomach to admit.

This is what I like to call the Goldilocks Theory of Marital Hell. She spends too much money. He doesn't make enough money. He won't get off his lazy ass and get a job. She wants him to take care of her. Somebody's porridge is always too hot and somebody's bed is always too soft. Oh well—at least something in the bed is soft.

Today, about 50 percent of marriages end in divorce. Why can't couples stay happily married and spend the rest of their lives together? As I mentioned earlier, my mother said you should never base your marriage on love alone, and I believe this is why so many marriages fail. A successful marriage is also based on money. Yes, I said it; I've crossed the politically correct line in the sand. But the fact remains that you should marry for money.

Take a deep breath and listen to a little logic. A marriage is basically a business. You have assets and liabilities; you meet someone else with assets and liabilities. Then you have to ascertain whether or not they are a good fit. No, I don't mean if his wanker is the size of a mule's or if her butt has the best sister wiggle you've ever seen. Those assets don't put money in the bank unless you belong to the local association of pimps and hos.

Just like any good business merger, you have to assess whether your goals are the same and if both parties get what they want out of the deal. The best part of marrying for money is that no one is in the dark as to anyone's intentions. I'm sure every person has seen the centerfold model hanging off the arm of a dried-up old millionaire. There's really no question who is getting what, and they obviously don't care what anyone thinks. Their merger is working. She will have money and status and potentially a great reward when he finally croaks; he gets the most luscious tits money can buy to rub his boys on until the day he dies.

"Oh, my God!" I can hear you say in shock. That is such a sordid arrangement—or is it? Every year Forbes releases its list of billionaires—not just the paltry millionaires, but the big boys and girls. Of the ninety-nine women on the Forbes 2008 Billionaire List, only ten were self-made. Fewer than twenty got it from their daddies, and the other seventy or so *married it*. Just because those women didn't spread their legs in the pages of a popular men's magazine (well, most of them) doesn't mean theirs was a story of star-crossed lovers.

Just for a moment imagine the life that could be yours if you somehow ascended into these ranks. Think about the designer clothing, exotic cars, yachts, and palatial mansions that would be at your disposal any time you wish. Your every desire is at your fingertips—or at least those of the maid or butler. Instead of the goose that laid a golden egg, you'd be laying the goose to get the golden egg.

Now just in case you think women have a much better chance at being treated like eye candy and doted on by a sugar daddy, remember that women live longer than men and tend to inherit the cash. This means there are literally hordes of wealthy widows just waiting to find a boy toy, and since most of these widows are fifty and older, any guy from a twenty-year-old to a retiree has a shot at the good life. How many men envy Ashton Kutcher, the modern face of the boy toy? Who cares if Demi is in her forties?

Before you let your hormones run amuck with excitement, it's important to remember that a marriage is a partnership no different than that found in business. Before we go any further, let me ask you a question: If you had a million dollars to open a restaurant, would you ask the first person you met that morning to be your partner? Of course not. What if this person didn't have any experience in the food service industry? How do you know about his or her work ethic? Indeed, you would look for someone who met your needs. I've been in several business partnerships over the course of my life, and I can tell you right now that if my business partner ran up our credit cards, lied to me about expenses, or didn't carry his or her own weight, our partnership would be dissolved.

So what tops the list when searching for that special someone with cash? I've listened to women claim that love conquers all while driving a rusted out Ford Pinto waiting for their husbands to get off the graveyard shift so they can eat breakfast at Denny's. I, however, pose this question: Does love really conquer all when you've worked the same crappy job for twenty-five years? Lived in the same house you've refinanced three times? When you have managed to venture only as far as the local go-kart races for a vacation? Is love strong enough to withstand years of financial struggle—only to end up destitute?

I'm not a gambling man by nature, but I'd be willing to bet that those women would prefer to be escorted to a five-star restaurant in Paris for dinner in a stretch limo rather than swat flies while they wolf down their ninety-nine-cent value menu McBurger. Forgive me for being frank but love doesn't pay the bills. Life is much better when you're rich. Money allows you to mitigate or eliminate most of life's problems and leaves your mind free to focus on the ones that really need your attention.

Had a bad day? No problem. There's a world-renowned spa waiting for you. Gained ten pounds? No need to exercise; just have a nip, tuck, and suck by the finest plastic surgeon. Just think of those poor bastards sweating away at the gym while your weight-loss program is only a scalpel away. Money makes life easier—and more fun.

CEO or Skanky Ho

At a dinner party one night during World War II, a drunken Winston Churchill asked an attractive woman whether she would sleep with him for a million pounds. "Maybe," the woman replied sheepishly. Intrigued, Churchill then asks, "Would you sleep with me for one pound?" The woman was taken aback by his comment and responded, "Of course not. What kind of woman do you think I am?" With drink in hand, Churchill cleverly replied, "Madam, we've already established what kind of woman you are. Now we're just negotiating the price."

The idea of marrying for money is something to which very few would admit, yet it happens all the time to varying degrees. It's considered a "negative" or morally reprehensible thing to do, but it is probably as old as—or older than—marriage itself.

Believe it or not, several studies have been conducted on this very subject, which just goes to show that I'm not alone in my stance about the price tag of marriage. One study found that the average "price" people would marry for is 1.5 million dollars. Just as the Churchill story relates, we've already determined what kind of people we are; now we're just negotiating the price.

So how much money do you want? A million and a half sounds like a lot of money but in reality it's not. More than likely, you'd still have to work and the thought of jetting across the globe to the hottest vacation spots is just that—a thought. Is it worth taking that wrinkled widow to dinner a couple of nights a week for a convertible BMW? Or is your time better suited going down on golden granny for a condo on the French Rivera, a cabin in Aspen, and a fleet of luxury sports cars?

Another important aspect to consider when marrying for money is how you want to be perceived. Do you want to be known as a pillar of the charity circuit? Bill Gate's wife helps him with his worldwide philanthropy and takes an active part in his business. Or do you want to be known as the chick who bagged a millionaire because she could open a beer bottle with her crotch, which brings us to Anna Nicole Smith. She married a man as old as Moses and counted the minutes until his last breath.

Once you hit the jackpot, though, you will soon be the topic of many conversations. Jealousy is such an ugly bug, and there will be those who are going to talk about how you married that person only for his or her money. They will talk about how they can't believe you would stoop so low. Just remember this: The entire time their lips are moving about what a letch you are, their mind is wishing they'd have gotten there first.

These days it isn't just the boob brigade who snags the millionaires; it's the smart chicks. You know—the ones who used to wear glasses and braces. Well, while you were drinking your way through college on the beer-or-bust plan, they were getting jobs that let them rub elbows—or whatever—with guys who would be millionaires.

And remember that there is no rule that a person with lots of money only gets to have one spouse. The only rule is one spouse *at a time*. All you have to do is get in line. Does it matter that you weren't first? No. In fact, most of the time it's better if you aren't. Why put up with someone who spends all their time making money? It is much better to find someone who has made his fortune already and is ready to spend it—on you.

The Lie of Love

Why are we so hung up on love anyway? When you dissect love it really is nothing more than a variety of emotions combined into one overwhelmingly addictive experience usually wrapped up in great sex. To me, love is like a burrito; you can fill it with anything you want, but you better be careful because before you know it you'll be squeezing your butt cheeks and hauling ass to the toilet because you ate too many refried beans. Just as your burrito has varying levels of spice, love has differing levels that can be applied to different people.

For example, you wouldn't answer the door in a leopard print thong with a woody the size of Texas if you knew it was your mother. Instead you'd scramble around your apartment, kicking beer cans under the sofa and slicking down your hair with your fingers before you answered the door.

Let's be honest: Do you really have sex with your spouse in the same way you would with a one-night stand you know you'll never see again? It's a little easier to get wild and nasty in a no-tell motel than it is in your master bedroom.

Love and sex aren't necessarily intertwined. You love your parents and siblings and other family members, don't you? You can't pick your family, but you love them just the same. This is proof you can love those with whom you have things in common. You don't have to feel the intoxicating emotion we usually refer to as love. So it stands to reason that if you find a millionaire with whom you share certain goals, you can learn to love him or her as well—especially if an eye-popping orgasm is part of the bargain.

This type of blissful union played out in many arranged marriages of old. Gandhi was married off in a match arranged by his family at the age of thirteen. The couple had five children and were married for more than sixty years. They were happy and loved each other—not over-the-top puppy love, but a deep and abiding understanding of one another. You can have the same thing with your rich partner.

Marrying for money isn't some sentence to a life void of emotion—just the opposite. You are free to understand and openly explore one another without fairytale expectations getting in the way. Many millionaires end up marrying their best friends of the opposite sex. They aren't inhuman; they need companionship and someone to talk to. Some of the highest-priced hookers on the planet will tell you that it is not uncommon for people with money to buy their time just to have someone to talk to—and many of those people married for "love."

> Marrying for money isn't some sentence to a life void of emotion—just the opposite. You are free to understand and openly explore one another without fairytale expectations getting in the way.

The problem with marrying in the throes of an emotional high is that it wears off like a bad sunscreen. You expose qualities in each other you didn't notice or just glossed over when you were bonking like bunnies in the early stages of sexual infatuation, which you confused with love. As the newness fades and the butterflies are killed off by your stomach acid, you start to become a little disillusioned. Add to this a string of financial woes, and you have a recipe for disaster.

It is often said that the line between love and hate is a thin one, but if love is so great then how can you so vehemently despise someone you once loved and for whom you would have given your very life? This is the power of our hormone-driven emotions. What you experienced wasn't real love. Love is about understanding and respect—not instant orgasms at the thought of their body. The sexual revolution has had a great deal to do with this phony idea of "love," but it was just an excuse to get your rocks off, not form a relationship that works.

Don't Question What Works

So this is the real deal. What do you want? Do you want a spouse who is on a hormone high, doesn't have a penny, and will be screwing a coworker a year from now? Do you want to worry about your retirement and scrape your dimes together at the end of every month to pay a disgruntled nurse's aide to wipe your butt and change your Depends? Or would you rather marry for money and find a long-term companion—with the added bonus of a sex buddy—with no ridiculous expectations?

Personally, I'd rather marry for money! You don't have to struggle though life if you team up with a person with cash and make your best deal. He or she is looking for one too. Once a person has assets, he or she wants to keep them. And every wealthy person knows that the easiest and

> You don't have to struggle though life if you team up with a person with cash and make your best deal.

fastest way to lose that fortune is to marry for love—and then divorce. This is because between the sheets, you don't think about prenups or protecting your assets. And that can get you in a real bind.

But…. But what? If you're feeling some twinge of moral reluctance, stop right now. Whose life is this anyway? Are you going to listen to old biddies who quilt all day, smell like Bengay, and have a refrigerator full of half-empty cat food cans? Or are you going to go out and seek to live the life you deserve? How many nights have you trolled the local bar looking for that one special person? How many times have you seen those same regulars perched on the same barstool, hoping you wouldn't end up just like them—hanging out, drinking, and taking home the losers who are left? There is nothing stopping you but you.

It takes just as much energy to marry a poor person as a rich one, and the benefits are substantially better if you go rich. Even if you think it's not that big a deal for you, what about your children and your family? Do you want your offspring (or potential offspring) to have the option of Harvard—or Redneck U? Do you want to spend your time at the premier parties on the East and West coasts, or spend your time at Podunk Holler potluck dinners and booster club meetings?

Your future is up to you; you just have to decide what you really want and then go get it. And it's easier than you think.

Throughout this book, I offer tips and techniques to take you from one of the crowd to one of the new rich through marriage. You may be a little hesitant at first to get completely on board with the idea, but once you understand the potential outcome, you will see the reality that marrying for money in today's financial environment is a necessity if you expect to live the life you deserve.

You can choose to have sex with a short bald average guy for the next twenty years, or you can have sex with a short bald millionaire (who can afford Viagra); it's up to you. All I'm saying is that if you have the choice, choose money. And we all have a choice.

The Real Fairytale Is Cash

Let's go back to Cinderella. Why would we create a story that makes it sound like love will bring a "happily ever after"? It's important to remember that history (and fairytales) was written by those who won, by those who accomplished their goals, and by those with money. So maybe we should take a closer look at the reality of her situation.

Picture a bitter and jealous scullery maid whose father married a woman in a typical arranged marriage of the time. The new wife was cunning and devious but gave it up on a regular basis and asked only that her two daughters be presented to men with money so as to increase the family wealth. The problem was that the husband died young, so his only daughter resented the new wife getting everything that was rightfully hers. Think about the fight between Anna Nicole and her dead husband's son, and you'll get the picture.

Now imagine that the smart and resourceful Cinderella has to find a way out of this mess. She has brains, and she knows how the rich think. She arranges a few coincidental meetings between herself and a rich prince. She even manages to let him rescue her and feel that testosterone rush through his veins. You guessed it—his dick gets hard and he has to have her.

This fair maiden hides from the prince's troops as they scour the countryside looking for her, and Cinderella then spreads rumors that the wicked stepmother locked her away. On the night of the ball, she sets her plan into motion, bringing in stylists and a designer gown—appearing in her finest at the ball and dazzling the prince's senses. She teases and taunts and strokes his ego and whatever else is begging to be petted, until she can get an arrangement in place. The two negotiate but are interrupted. She leaves just enough clues for him to find her, but not enough to make it easy—just like the woman who leaves the tube of lipstick or unique earrings but no phone number.

After whacking off at her memory for weeks, he'll do anything to have her—including giving her half his kingdom (community property, you know). With the deal imminent, she allows him to find her and before the stepmother can get her girls into pasties and G-strings, Cinderella has stolen the prize and flips them the bird as the fairytale coach rolls into the sunset.

Cinderella didn't marry for love; she married for money and set out not just to be a player but to emerge the winner. The only reason we think of Cinderella as a deserving and worthy princess is simple: Cinderella played the game and won. Sorry for shattering the mirror of illusion. But life is no fairytale, my friend. The practical and the mundane always take their toll.

Let's head outside the ballroom so you too can understand the unspoken rules of the marrying for money game.

Summary

℃ Marrying for love is a relatively new phenomenon.

℃ Arranged marriages worked because they were based on common financial goals that benefited both families.

℃ In order to find true, lasting happiness, marriage must also be treated as a business arrangement or merger.

℃ Basing a relationship on fleeting emotions and sexual infatuation (erroneously called love) is unpredictable and uncertain, and fuels the escalating divorce rate.

℃ Many of today's billionaires married someone with little to no monetary assets.

℃ It takes as much energy to marry a poor person as a rich one but the benefits are vastly different.

Two: Love Don't Pay the Bills

If love is blind, why is lingerie so popular?—*Unknown*

AH, SWEET LOVE. THERE'S SOMETHING about falling in love that makes our nerves tingle and pulses race. The minute we think we've meet the "one," our world turns inside out. Instantly our fingers turn into an abacus as we count every waking second until we get to see this person again. Life is wonderful. Rain clouds morph into little lambs skipping through the sky. Mother Nature paints her beautiful canvas with brilliant colors.

The guy struts around town like he just scored the winning touchdown and nailed the head cheerleader. His perpetual woody is marching at attention. Women are no different. Hovered together in a gaggle gossiping about where they went to dinner or how good he is in bed. Their rock hard nipples enter the room and demand attention. The two are drawn together just like a divining rod to a puddle of water. The hustle and bustle of the day is of no consequence because you know later that evening, you'll be wrapped in your loved one's arms. War, world hunger, and all the bad in the universe disappear once Cuddly Wuddly is giving it to you from behind.

This may seem like an exaggeration, but there is a kernel of truth in how irrational our behavior becomes when we fall in love. What makes the attraction so intense to cause you to lose your mind and ignore those annoying and often financially devastating little details? In large part it is physical. He looks like a Greek God. Her cleavage makes you want to cram your face (or whatever) deep inside. All of us like to think we are attracted to the right person and life will be wonderful, but the truth is that most of us spend more time trolling gas station parking lots looking to save two cents per gallon than we do searching for Mr. or Ms. Right. We stumble across someone at a bar, at work, or at the grocery store, and next thing you know, we're bedded and wedded—and all because we were convinced we were in "love."

Falling in love isn't hard. In fact, it is a completely spontaneous experience that can happen at any time. You don't have to do anything. That's why it's called "falling" in love—because it's happening to you without any conscious thought on your part. I'm sure you've heard someone say something similar to this: "There I was just standing all alone and he came along and just swept me off my feet." (Just a side note: It's more effective if you say it in a southern drawl, à la Scarlett O'Hara) Think about the imagery of that statement. It implies that you were just standing there, doing nothing, and then something came along and happened to catch you by surprise and knock you down. You know, a hurricane or tornado can do the same thing. Sweep you off of your feet and drop you on your butt leaving you dazed and confused.

When you think about it, humans were made for one-night stands, not fifty years of drudgery. It is Mother Nature's intention for us to procreate, not for us to fall in love forever and always—just for right now. Monogamy isn't natural, so why complicate matters with love? Whether you're young and naïve or wrinkled and incontinent, divorced for the umpteenth time or a vestal virgin searching for the one with the key to your chastity belt, your body reacts to the visual signals making you loins quiver, your heart race, and your hands sweat—which, by the way, saves you from having to use lube.

We've all felt this blood-pumping, heat-pounding need for a star-studded cock ring or a twelve-inch veiny dildo. It's no wonder the adult toy industry has exploded (pardon the pun) over the past few years. More often than not, we translate this shared physical response into a deep connection that fills us with new and wondrous emotions to explore. We revel in the sheer wonder of the other person. Not about one thing in particular but simply in the idea that he or she exists. It's pretty amazing considering a month earlier you may have passed this person on the sidewalk and not cared if he or she existed or not. But now it's like seeing this person naked for the first time, but not just seeing with your eyes, but with your hands, your mouth, your whole body and being. You throw him or her on the bed, all the nerves in your body standing on end. All because of this overwhelming feeling we call love.

When the Stains Dry

So what happens the morning after? Are you still in love? Does his or her morning breath singe the hair on your head? Can you still see yourself spending the rest of your life with this person? Unless the sex was so bad you wanted to sew your head to the carpet, more than likely your answer is yes. Before you rush out and look for wedding rings based on this feeling, I want you to carefully consider what I'm about to tell you. Love is not a feeling. The only thing you're feeling is the afterglow of the adrenalin high. Falling in love is nothing more than a momentary flash of emotions. How hot will you feel when you find out he or she has 36,000 dollars' worth of credit card debt? That'll shrivel up that afterglow and a whole lot more. It won't take you long to realize that life is completely different with a wealthy and generous partner, and it has nothing to do with how hot he or she is in bed.

When you were young, did your parents teach you never to make a rash decision based on emotions? I remember taking my daughter to look for a car for her sixteenth birthday. We spent three months' worth of Saturdays at the car dealerships, looking for the perfect vehicle. Each time she'd see a different car, she squealed with delight and said, "Oh, Daddy, this is the one. I love this car. This is the car I've wanted my whole life. Please, can I have this car?" A few blocks later, "Oh, Daddy, I know I said I liked that other car, but this one is totally the one. I love this car. I'll just die if I don't get this. Please. Please." As you may have guessed, six months later she was complaining that her car wasn't cool enough.

Often, many of us go into marriage with this same sense of urgency: We'll just die if we don't spend the rest of our lives with that certain someone only to find ourselves wanting to blow our brains out a couple of years later if we have to look at this person for another second. Well, there's the "falling" feeling in falling in love. Why? Because it feels like we have no choice in the matter. Something strikes us like a bolt of lightning, and down we go. Love is nothing more than a strong attraction to a person. In the early stages, we usually fall in love with long blonde hair, muscular chest, or sense of humor. Guess what, folks? Life has a way of turning hair gray, melting muscles into flab, and replacing that pleasant smile with a grimace.

The more two people get to know each other, the more comfortable they become and the less sharp, bright, and exciting the falling in love experience is. This is true in all relationships. In the beginning, you fell in love, anticipated his or her call, wanted to spend every waking moment with him or her, and basically made everyone around you want to barf. This person's idiosyncrasies were so cute and endearing. But after a few years of marriage, the euphoria of love fades. Slowly but surely, those calls just to say "I love you" drive you insane. You put your phone on vibrate and ignore it. You cringe at the thought of their touch, and sex becomes a way to shut them up rather than fulfill a need. And those sweet idiosyncrasies soon will annoy the ever living shit out of you. Trust me on this one, folks; eventually he or she will piss you off to the point that you want to scrub the toilet with his or her toothbrush.

The symptoms of this stage vary with every relationship, but stop for a moment and think about the difference between newlyweds and couples who've been married for several years. If you've ever eaten dinner at a restaurant before 4:30 (especially if you live in Florida and they offer a two-for-one special) you'll see a barrage of old couples wallowing in their self-induced misery. There is definitely a dramatic difference between the initial "love" stage and the rest of the relationship, and making sure you have the finances taken care of gives you a much higher chance of staying in the relationship.

Is This You?

When you got married, you knew your spouse-to-be didn't make a lot of money, but you were in love and willing to accept a life without extravagances. As time passed, however, and you began to see all the opulence others had, you secretly wanted more. But you continued on in your marriage thinking you were happy, until through a sister, a friend, a cousin—the who really doesn't matter—you caught a glimpse of how much easier life can be. Now you've become secretly, overwhelmingly envious because they married into an insane amount of dough and just like that, they have everything you will work your whole life for and probably still never have.

You resent how much better their standard of living is than yours. They don't have to check their bank balance online before they go to the store; they don't have to choose generic shampoo or eat macaroni and cheese or ramen noodles for weeks on end to make ends meet. They don't have to squirm in front of a banker trying to get a loan for a house with a leaky roof and toilet that runs.

They have their own mortgage-free mansion, a substantial trust fund, and the world at their fingertips. While you, on the other hand, schlep your butt to the same job day after day, shop at Wal-Mart, and rotate Hamburger Helper between Mondays and Wednesdays each week. They don't have to work, you do. They get to go to brunch, get massages, and spend their days doing whatever feels good at the time. Your days are divided between school pick-up, PTA meetings, and ridiculous projects for a job you hate. Their spouses are extremely wealthy, and now you get to sit back and fume over the fact that they are the beneficiaries of all that wealth.

Jealousy soon crowds your emotions, leaving less and less room for "love." The envy demon pokes you with his pitch-fork every waking second of the day. Your husband/wife is a fantastic parent, and you very much appreciate how he or she loves you, but you can't help but start to believe that there's more to life than being a good spouse and parent. On your thirtieth birthday, you got a card, cake, and dinner at Red Lobster, while your secret arch nemesis had a fabulous trip to Rome, a silver Porsche, and another maid to feed the yippy good-for-nothing Chihuahua whose ruby-studded collar cost more than your first car.

While their family vacations last three months and traverse twelve countries, yours is another week at Yellowstone shower-ing beneath a freezing stream of water in a park campground. They have *foie gras* and fancy wine, and you have sandwiches from the picnic basket your dog peed on. You pretend to be thrilled for them, but you are sick with envy. You wish you had married for money so you could enjoy the finer things in life. Resentment races up your spine at every holiday dinner or social gathering. You have to stab your leg with a fork to keep from shouting, "I hate my life!" Love is all fine and dandy, but there is a lot to be said about a villa in the south of France and a staff to take care of the day-to-day details.

There's a story I heard that sums up that stage of a relation-ship when you realize marrying for money is a valid idea:

A gorgeous young woman took her rich husband to the doctor's office. After his examination, the doctor told the wife,

"If you don't do the following, your husband will surely die. Each morning, fix him a healthy breakfast and send him off to the country club in a good mood. At lunchtime, make him a hot, nutritious meal and put him in a good frame of mind before he takes his afternoon nap. For dinner, fix an especially nice meal and don't burden him with household chores. Have sex with him several times a week and satisfy his every whim."

On the way home, the husband asked the wife, "What did the doctor say honey?"

She replied, "He said you're going to die."

Jones'n for Love

Remember the anti-drug commercials that compared a frying egg to your brain on marijuana? Did you know that love is a drug? And no, I'm not referring to some eighties new wave song? We've all seen how goofy people act when they're in love. They walk around all day smiling like they've just discovered the secret to life. Have you ever wondered why? Love birds roam around, oblivious to their surroundings—much like junkies walking around looking for the next hit.

When we are attracted to another person, our systems are flooded with chemicals that give us a high like none other. It's like an ongoing orgasm. When you're in love, your brain is flooded with dopamine. This feel-good chemical makes us float around in a sense of euphoria. Dopamine is a neurotransmitter and causes the body to respond to stimuli. Cocaine also stimulates dopamine so the high is similar and so is your reaction to it. Your brain craves that feeling, and once you get a taste of it, you only want more. Have you ever wondered why you screw like rabbits during those first few months and stay up talking until the wee hours of the night—but you still have plenty of energy during the day? That's your brain—your brain on dopamine.

People in love notice less need for sleep, extra energy, and decreased appetite. This should also sound familiar to the side effects of amphetamines and cocaine, which also alter the mind in large part by raising dopamine levels. The downside of high dopamine levels is anxiety, restlessness, and depression. When you are in "love," this might manifest itself in a stream of thoughts running through your head that sound something like this for women:

"I can't wait for him to call!" Stares at phone. "Ring, damn it! His dimples are just the cutest thing and he is so funny! I've never been around anyone so funny. And we have so much in common—he likes purple slushies, I like purple slushies." Picks up the phone and checks for a dial tone. "And he has great plans and is really smart. The car wash gig is just temporary he's really going places. *Why won't that phone ring?*"

Of course, it's different for men and may sound something like this:

"Has it been long enough for me to call?" Combs hair for the fifth time. "She was so hot out on that dance floor and those luscious boobs taste great!" Smells shirt. "Her laugh makes me harder than a rock. On that dance floor last night everyone was watching her and she was with *me!*" Checks watch. "Don't blow it, dude; another five minutes and then you can call."

Everything else goes by the wayside as you obsess on getting more and more of that feeling—more of the dopamine high. Just like a drug addict. You find yourself on the edge emotionally and bounce from elation to depression with the ups and downs. One minute you're high as a kite, the next you're crying your eyes out.

Dopamine interferes with our ability to concentrate and control our thoughts, so elevated dopamine levels could explain lovers' tendencies to focus exclusively on their beloved. Often these crazy feelings become intertwined with our "emotional high" in the throes of passion. Scary. The relationship can turn on a dime. They love you. They hate you. They want to hold you. They want to cut your head off. Remember *Fatal Attraction?* I don't think any of us wants to come home to the Easter Bunny bubbling away on the stove, but it can happen when someone is on a dopamine high.

It's clear to anyone who has been in love—and fallen out of love—that people in this state are incapable of making a rational decision because they are out of their frickin' minds. Would you let a meth head invest your money? Not if you wanted to keep it. Yet most people make one of the most important decisions of their life while under the influence of this dopamine-induced emotional volatility.

Still not convinced?

Actual scientists, not just men who play them on TV, have determined that the feeling we know as love has a lifespan of two years (well, more like eighteen months). Scientists from the University of Pisa in Italy found that the levels of oxytocin, which they deemed the "cuddle hormone," decline after a period of approximately two years. (Oxytocin is a chemical known to induce labor and milk production in pregnant women and new mothers.) After this time span, the chemical that makes new lovers irresistible to each other seems to disappear from their systems. They also found a nerve growth factor called neurotrophins exceeded normal levels in those enjoying the love struck early stages of romance.

> Scientists from the University of Pisa in Italy found that the levels of oxytocin, which they deemed the "cuddle hormone," decline after a period of approximately two years.

One particular study took blood samples from several couples—both young and old—at various stages in their relationships, both young and old. These different hormones were present in the samples taken from the newlyweds whereas there was no evidence of the same hormones in people who had been in a stable relationship for many years. As a matter of fact, the study showed that some of these love molecules (and no, I'm not referring to the ones on the hotel bedspread) can disappear as early as twelve months after new love sweeps you off your feet.

Knowing this, would you be willing to risk your financial

future on a temporary and fleeting emotion? To me, this is no different than cashing in your retirement money and heading to Las Vegas. Only you don't sit at the poker tables where you actually have a chance at winning; instead you take your entire life savings, stroll over to the Roulette table, and plop it all down on thirty-three black. Do you know the odds of winning? None too good, my friend, none too good. Neither are the odds of your infatuation-based marriage lasting based on this new research.

Falling in love has been linked to other hormonal changes too. Researchers in Italy who studied serotonin and love affairs compared hormone levels of people recently in love and those who were single or in a long-term relationship. They found that women who had recently fallen in love had higher testosterone levels than those who had not recently fallen in love, and men in love had lower testosterone than those who were not. Both men and women who had recently fallen in love also had higher levels of the stress hormone cortisol. When researchers tested these people again one to two years later, their hormone levels were no longer different from those not in a relationship.

Since the "in-love" stage of a relationship typically lasts six to eighteen months and occasionally as long as three years, why are so many people sealing their doom by becoming bride and groom? Are you honestly willing to accept your fate with the hopes you can just get used to your spouse? As you can see from the scientific studies as well as the other information in this chapter, a lifelong sustainable love is next to impossible.

It is interesting to me how the prevalence of "dating" online has grown. The most popular sites are those that ask you dozens (or hundreds) of questions and match you with people based on "compatibility." Of course, one of those areas of compatibility is financial. You have to have the same goals and interests financially in order for any relationship to be possible. So the idea of marrying for money is responsible and well thought out—not immoral!

You will actually have a better chance of being happy and staying married to someone with common interests than you will with that guy in accounting you met at the water cooler last week. Let go of your preconceived ideas, sugar-coated fantasies, and hormone-induced hallucinations, and we'll explore how marrying for money can be one of the best deals you ever had.

Pardon Me; I Knew I Shouldn't Have Eaten Those Enchiladas

Now I'm going to take you on a journey to a land far far way and ask you to delve deeply into your mind and pull from your memory one of your very first dates. Not just any date, but one in which you were stark raving mad about this person. Have one in mind? Good; now play along with me. The two of you are home on the couch kissing after a fabulous dinner at Jorge's Cantina. The kisses get deeper, and before you know it your clothes are in a wad on the floor. The night is almost perfect with one exception: The side of refried beans you ordered. As you roll around on the sofa in ecstasy, your butt cheeks are squeezed together tight enough to incinerate a concrete cinderblock. As your neck is being kissed, you say a silent prayer of panic: "Please don't let me fart. I promise, I'll go to church every Sunday, help children in third world countries, and volunteer all my spare time with lepers."

We are all human. Each of us toot, poot, and barf. Rich people take dumps just like the rest of us. Granted they probably have a butler standing there to wipe, but they poop just the same. For some crazy reason, people assume that to court the rich, you have to become a paragon of etiquette of whom Miss Manners would be proud. Nothing can be further from the truth. Bodily functions know no boundaries. Don't assume that lack of experience or knowledge keeps you out of the game.

You don't have to fake anything (except maybe an orgasm or two) or be something you aren't to hook up with Mr. or

Ms. loaded. You can and must be yourself. If you cater to or kiss up to someone with money, they will view you as nothing more than the help. Maids and butlers get laid, but they don't get married.

Cardinal rule number one: The only difference between you and a rich person is the size of your bank account. They aren't really any different than you are (although some of them might think so). They raid the fridge after the help goes to bed, spy on the next door neighbor sunbathing in the nude, and get just as pissed when the bank charges them fees (maybe even more so). I've been around millionaires who spent twenty minutes on the phone with their bank getting a two-dollar charge reversed, so believe me when I tell you they have their own little oddities just like anyone else.

So what do you have in common with someone who has money? To find this answer, let's go back to the *Forbes* billionaire list for 2008. Fewer than 20 percent of the people on that list inherited their wealth. Everyone else represents first-generation money. That means they were raised on farms, in city flats, in the suburbs, or even the inner city. You probably have more in common with them than the people they are currently around each day, and you can give them the opportunity to be themselves instead of trying to fit the "rich" mold into which they've contorted themselves. This is also why many of these newly wealthy are attracted to mates without the glitter. Authentic people feel familiar and remind them of a simpler time in their lives. My uncle used to say, no matter how much perfume you slather on a pig, it's still just a pig. These rich people don't have to come home and pretend to know (or care) which wine goes with duck or who the newest socialite is; they can be themselves.

You don't have to take a one-hundred-question quiz to know what you want out of life. In fact, this approach is backward. It centers on the idea that you take what already exists and then find someone who fits that mold. You have the ability to create the life you want and change anything in it so it stands to reason that the best approach is to create a list of how you want your life to be—rather than listing how it is—and then create the life you desire. Why put a round peg in a square hole, so to speak?

Rich Is as Rich Does

If you want to get to know someone rich, and he or she wants to get to know someone like you, then why haven't you come across a whole slew of them? There are several reasons, but the main problem is the company you keep. All of us belong to a set circle of contacts—our families, our friends, our business associates. It stands to reason that if this circle doesn't contain a large percentage of wealthy individuals, your odds of meeting a single millionaire to marry goes way down. And don't think that billionaires—or millionaires for that matter—are only located in New York or Los Angeles. They are everywhere! They are doctors, lawyers, real estate investors, oil moguls, and retail magnates, just to name a few.

This doesn't mean you have to kick your friends and family to the curb, just that you should expand your circle of contacts to include those who know wealthy people. Notice I didn't say to expand it to include wealthy people; that can be tough as they won't know you from Adam. The trick is to gain introduction to their world through people who know them. For instance, Realtors in the luxury home market, travel specialists, and even private airplane pilots can give you an introduction to the world of wealth.

I recently saw a reality TV show whose premise is to match up millionaires who didn't have time to meet people. I, of course, recognized the real principle, which is introducing to the wealthy people interested in being with a millionaire. Some of the potential candidates even specified how many millions the other had to have in order for them to go to the trouble of dating!

You would think everyone would love to have money, but it is surprising how many people feel more virtuous or "normal" without it. They seem to think that money changes you, which is not true; it just makes you more of what you already are. I encounter people on a daily basis who believe that to want money, or a better life, means they are discounting or deserting their values and their past. This kind of all-or-nothing thought process just convinces you to do what's expected and struggle through life like everyone else. The problem is, everyone else isn't struggling. There are tens of thousands of millionaires who are living wonderful, comfortable lives, and there is no reason why you cannot join those ranks. You can choose your life—and suffering is optional.

> There are tens of thousands of millionaires who are living wonderful, comfortable lives, and there is no reason why you cannot join those ranks.

The biggest difference between you and the millionaires next door is in the way they think. They focus on making more money—they don't obsess over paying bills or wondering if they will fit in with the "rich" crowd. You may think it's something that happens over time as they get more and more cash, but the reality is that they always had this mindset and you can too. In order for this idea of marrying for money to work for you, you have to stop stressing about what you don't have, what you don't like, and what you don't know. You can't worry what people might think; what is important is reaching your own goals and making your dreams come true.

Shared Interest

Not long ago I met a woman—let's call her Angela—who was appalled I promoted the idea of marrying for money. So I asked Angela, who is married to a wealthy oil man, how she and her husband came to know each other. Turns out she met him at the office; she was an executive assistant. She supported his business and came to know him better than almost anyone as they spent so many hours together. They fell in "love" and were married. (I wonder how many of those "loving" embraces were on the corporate conference table after hours?) She went on to tell me that her husband was the kind of man she'd always dreamed of marrying, and I'm sure she's sincere.

Of course, if he hadn't had a dime to his name, he probably wouldn't have even turned her head. So they never would have gotten to the "love" stage, and the fact she quit working the second she said "I do" confirms that there's more going on than she's admitting. She may think she didn't marry for money, but I know better. And if I've learned anything it's that the holier-than-thou crowd are only offended by things they have done but which they don't want to admit. Angela's story points to the fact that having a shared and common goal is a solid basis for a lasting relationship.

It's interesting that relationships based on shared interests and common goals can survive problems and issues that would sink a marriage based on love alone. Take, for example, Bill and Hillary Clinton. Their common political goals are of primary importance, and they openly state that as one of the reasons their marriage has overcome failure, infidelity, and media scrutiny. Businesspeople often hook up with like-minded mates. Bill Gates's wife worked for him as a Microsoft manager. Carl Icahn's second wife was his long-time assistant Gail. These people were in the same location, focusing on the same goals, and helping their rich and talented partners get what they want. At the same time, they were getting what they wanted—and you can too.

Summary

- ☾ Most people spend more time trying to save 2 cents per gallon on gasoline than trying to find Mr. or Ms. Right.
- ☾ Humans were designed for one-night stands, not year-after-year drudgery.
- ☾ Falling in love is just a flash of fleeting emotions, not

something to bet your financial future on.

(Love doesn't cure all but it certainly takes care of most of the details in life.

("Love" is dopamine-induced euphoria, and not a state of mind in which to make life-defining decisions.

(Don't let lack of experience or knowledge keep you out of the game.

(You can choose your life—and suffering is optional.

(Common vision and common goals have greater sticking power than hormonally prompted infatuations.

Three: Diggin' for Gold

No gold-digging for me...I take diamonds! We may be off the
gold standard someday.—*Mae West*

IF YOU WANT TO GO SNOW SKIING, YOU wouldn't hop on a
plane to the Caribbean, would you? So it doesn't make much
sense to work hard, play the stock market, or build a business
from the ground floor in an attempt to become instantly rich.
Why not take a different route? Robert Frost's famous poem *The
Road Not Taken* answers this question quite well: "I took the one
less traveled by, and that has made all the difference." Why not
venture down a path less traveled? Perhaps a path leading down
the aisle? Yes, I'll admit, it's not politically correct to go on the
prowl for a marital meal ticket, but the truth of the matter is
money makes the world go 'round. If money is important to
you, then just tell the truth (to yourself) and make it a part of
your life's design and your search for a mate.

I'm talking about real money. Not just someone who has
a cabin in Steamboat Springs or a condo in West Palm. I'm
referring to a mogul who owns a private island complete with
staff and yacht. Who doesn't want immense wealth? Hundred-
dollar bills in your small change pocket, multiple mansions,
jewelry, personal jet, A-list parties, Christmas in Vail, and
everything else that money can buy? Money has the ability to
help you overlook his "dicky do" disability (where his stomach
sticks out further than his dicky do) or to ignore that snack-size
Yorkie she dresses in cashmere and carries in her purse. When
you're financially fabulous, life is much more fun and exciting,
so much so, in fact, that money has become one of the most
important factors in today's world.

Any boy toy wearing a ten-karat diamond pinkie ring to his wife's thirty-year high school reunion who says, "It's not really about the money" is a big fat liar. Women who stand by their millionaire husband's side professing their love for him despite the fact that he has an affinity for transvestite hookers in stilettos aren't fooling anybody either. The only love in that marriage is for his fluffy bank account. I guarantee you if they were poor and lived in a trailer, that trannie's high heel would've been shoved up his butt a long time ago. Cold hard cash makes all the difference in the world of matrimony.

Let's be practical. We all want a huge mansion, a garage full of exotic sports cars, vacations to locations across the globe, and the means to do whatever you want when you want. I don't think this is too much to ask, do you? You're going to have to live in some sort of a house and drive some sort of a car—unless you're a glutton for punishment and use public transportation—so why not live in a showplace overlooking the ocean and drive a Porsche?

Let me ask you a few questions before we go any further.

Would you rather live in squalor or in splendor?

Armani or Goodwill?

Bargain-bin fighting over the last thong or a private shopper paying full price without a care in the world?

When most people think about the rich and famous, Beverly Hills instantly comes to mind. After all, there was even a television show about seven spoiled brats—and one wannabe—living in 90210. The median income in 2007 for Beverly Hills was 129,824 dollars. By most people's standards that is a pretty nice chunk of change. But is it enough to keep up with the proverbial Joneses? Let's see…at a minimum, you're going to need a decent-sized home with a pool, BMW convertible, and a membership to one of the many exclusive golf and tennis clubs. In case you don't have a calculator handy, let me add up those expenses for you.

House: $2 million   Payment: $20,000/month
Car: $40,000   Payment: $790/month
Club memberships: $60,000   Payment: $5,000/month
                      Total expenses: $25,790/month

With your monthly income of 10,810 dollars (and that's before taxes), you're not anywhere close to making enough money to live the lifestyle you want and deserve. This lavish lifestyle is putting you deep into debt. How does that song go? "Another day older and deeper in debt"? What's worse, if you are like most of America, you're going to need at least ten times what you currently make to live in a reasonable level of comfort.

How much money do you make in a year? Forty, fifty, sixty thousand dollars? Not too shabby—downtown loft, nice car, closet full of the latest fashion, a few credit card payments. And after socking away a couple hundred bucks a month, you and your sweetheart can go to Cancun next spring. Sounds good, right? It won't for long. Let's compare your 50,000-dollar-a-year salary to someone who makes 43 million dollars a year. If you break these salaries down to hourly wages, you make roughly 25 dollar an hour while Mr. or Ms. Millionaire makes 21,500 dollars per hour. So again, let me ask you this: What do you think about marrying for money?

In the eighties and nineties we used to carry a condom in our wallet or purse just to be on the safe side. But today our need for protection goes far beyond worrying about catching some dreaded disease. The next time you go to happy hour with the intent of finding the love of your life, ask to see a financial statement before anyone buys you a drink. If you're truly intent on marrying for money, go above and beyond in investigating the potential candidates. Google is a wonderful tool for this sort of inquiry. All sorts of juicy information is just waiting to be discovered. You see, we *want* love, but we *expect* money.

It's All About You

Now that you've agreed that this is indeed a brilliant idea, you may be wondering how realistic it is to meet—much less marry—a millionaire or billionaire. Before I reveal the hot spots for finding your potential gold-encrusted bride or groom, you first need to understand the fundamental cornerstone of this process. Marrying into the jet set depends only on your mindset.

Several years ago my family had a cookout. We were sitting on the deck discussing such important topics as which water sealer did my brother-in-law use and how much the trees had grown. My niece Caroline, who was five at the time, wanted very badly to get in on the conversation. The more we talked, the harder she tried to join in. The poor kid couldn't get a word in edgewise. After pacing back and forth several hundred times, she marched right into the middle of us, stomped her foot, and said, "I want to talk! It's all about me!" Many would think this is a selfish thing to say, but I have to admit the little lady figured it out early on. It *is* all about you. Nobody else has your best interest at heart. Only you do.

You and *your* happiness should always come first. The bane of our existence is to fulfill our own needs. The Dalai Lama stated it best: "The purpose of life is to be happy." True happiness, living a joyful life with financial success. Darwin was right. It is about survival of the fittest. No one can make you happy but you, and you can't live for someone else or fulfill someone else's needs without first taking care of yours. Securing our financial future should be the ultimate goal for every one of us.

Why is this important? Our society values money. It has been ingrained in our minds as how we place value on ourselves.

If you've ever uttered the words, "I can't spend that much money on myself," then you have to ask why not? Aren't you worth it? You would spend it on someone else, wouldn't you? So value yourself by buying something only you will use and you will benefit from. Try a massage, a new outfit, or a day doing nothing but splurging on yourself. The first step is changing your perspective. Make yourself your top priority. Work will still be there tomorrow. If you're lucky, you'll meet Mr. or Ms. Moneybags and be able to quit your job. Your friends and family won't leave; they will still be in the same spot as yesterday.

Believe it or not if you don't have the right mindset about money, your life will never change. Sadly, most people believe that "other people" become rich and have everything they want in life. Even with the best intentions and a foolproof plan to "accidentally" meet a millionaire, many won't bag the bucks. Why? Because of their financial mindset. Your emotions create your thoughts, and your thoughts either cause you to act or prevent you from acting. If you don't believe you are worthy of money, you're preventing yourself from taking action to meet and marry your financial future.

No ifs, ands, or buts about it—every one of us deserves to be rich. And don't make the mistake of assuming you can't have this mindset until you are wealthy. Everyone has to start somewhere. Self-made millionaires possessed this attitude when they first started out. Just because you do not have a substantial bank account at the moment, does not mean that without some hard work and determination your mindset couldn't get you there—via the altar. In all honesty, this way of thinking is more valuable than any level of education or bank account size. It is the reason why many millionaires and billionaires who lose their fortune are able to regain their wealth again. Donald Trump is a great example of this; he lost tons of money through a string of divorces and some bad real estate investments. Losses of this magnitude could knock an ordinary man down, but not "the Donald." He has the right attitude. He knows the ins and outs and the how to live the life of the rich and famous. You too need to develop this line of thought. In the words of George Bernard Shaw, "It's a sin to be poor."

Billionaire Business Basics 101

Marrying for money is one of the oldest gigs on the planet. As I mentioned in the first chapter, marriages were often arranged for monetary gain. You can't search for your financial security halfheartedly. You need to stay on top of your game. In your current job, you can't show up when you feel like it, take two hours for lunch, and leave early every Friday. Your boss would boot you out on your butt in the blink of an eye. No, you have to be punctual, professional, and willing to go the extra mile. Marrying for money is no different. This is a business—and it's not for the faint of heart.

Your pedigree, upbringing, and current living situation have no bearing on your chances to marry into money. You could have been conceived in the backseat of a rusted-out Camero, raised in a double wide, and worked at every Dairy Queen and Tastee Freeze across the country—and it still wouldn't hurt your chances to marry into wealth. All you need is determination, intent, drive, and desire for a better life. Since this is a business, you need to understand that there are going to be a few expenses. After all, no company can run without operating capitol. Don't worry; once you land your target, you'll never have to worry about money again. Below, I've listed a few necessary items for your business:

- ☾ *Wardrobe.* Be prepared. You never know when you might get the last-minute invitation to go skiing. Make sure you have enough clothes to cover a variety of occasions from galas, conventions, cocktail parties, formal dinners, and a leisurely day at the beach.
- ☾ *Gym membership/personal trainer.* Put down the Twinkie! After you have the wedding ring, you can eat all the cream-filled delights you want.
- ☾ *Weekly/biweekly grooming.* (More on this later)
- ☾ *Savings account for any plastic surgery and other anti-aging treatments.* Youth fades but BOTOX goes on forever.

Think of yourself as a one man/woman show—your own personal corporation. I compare this to scanning the classifieds for a job. You don't even read most of the ads because you know the work and pay aren't worth your time. Imagine the wealthy as a giant classified ad section; scan the list and consider only those who can offer the best compensation. As any entrepreneur knows—never undervalue your services.

It is important to seek creative solutions to any obstacles. The following story illustrates this concept:

An elderly couple went to a local doctor. The doctor asked, "What can I do for you?"

The man replied, "Will you watch us make love?"

The doctor looked puzzled but agreed. When the couple had finished, the doctor said, "There is nothing wrong with the way you do it." And he charged them 32 dollars.

This happened several weeks in a row. The couple would schedule an appointment; make love, pay the doctor, and leave. Finally, the doctor asked, "Just exactly what are you trying to find out?"

The old man said, "We're not trying to find out anything. She's married, so we can't go to her house. I'm married so we can't go to my house. The Holiday Inn charges 60 dollars and the Hilton charges 78 dollars. We do it here for 32 bucks, and I get 28 dollars from Medicare for a doctor's visit."

Don't ever lose sight of what you want—but watch that bottom line!

Ooh-La-La or Oh My God!

Do you remember that Vidal Sassoon commercial with the beautiful woman whisking her hair around while the announcer's voice booms in the background saying, "Vidal Sassoon. If you don't look good, we don't look good"? Well, it's time for brutal honesty; it doesn't matter how beautiful you are on the inside, but if you look like a creature from another planet, you may get a little late night nookie, but you're never going to get a wedding ring. It's not fair, but face it: In this culture, looks are everything. Nobody wants to walk into a party with Sasquatch on their arm. Take a moment and think about the last reunion you attended. Did you stress over your looks? Try to drop a quick twenty pounds? I know of a group of thirtysomethings who all decided to have some sort of plastic surgery before their twenty-year reunion. They even made their husbands go on diets and rented a stretch limo for the big night. Why? Because looks are important.

Gone are the days when skin treatments, plastic surgery, and perfume were considered only for women. More than ever, men too are concerned about their looks; they are hitting the gym and spending big bucks on skin care, fashion, and hair care.

A man loves a woman with a good body. There's nothing like the feeling of having a beautiful woman by your side with a body that screams for attention and gets it. It's the same feeling women have when they walk into a room with a fine, handsome man and the whole crowd stares at him. Everyone is a sucker for a beautiful person. It's our weakness. But beauty doesn't just happen; you have to work at it. Before you set out to meet your millionaire, remember these important tips.

Hair. Wax on, wax off. The only place hair belongs is on your head. And yes, this goes for the guys too. A smooth clean body is sexy. It is a total turnoff for your nether regions to feel like steel wool. And there is nothing worse than having to use a weed whacker to trim your bush, if you know what I mean. Gray hair is also a big no-no—anywhere on your body. There is always the risk of being traded in for a younger model, so keep an eye out for any smoke in the stack.

Teeth. White and straight. I can't emphasize this enough. Your teeth are one of the first things people see, and yellow dingy teeth give an instant bad impression. Yuck mouth is a total turnoff, and these days, an instant assumption that you were once a meth addict! If your smile looks like a Halloween Jack O'Lantern, for God's sake get them fixed.

Skin. Three words. Zip, suck, and tuck. The only thing that should dangle when you wave, dance, or get some booty is jewelry. Pasty white went out with the French aristocracy, so buy some tan in a bottle and give yourself a rub down. Stay out of the sun; you don't want to waste your newfound millions on radiation and chemotherapy.

Unmentionables. No funky monkey. Keep 'em clean. Enough said.

Nails. Neat and shaped. Scraggly nails, on both fingers and toes, are not only disgusting to look at, but can also cause harm. Many a pair of pantyhose fell victim to the snag of an unruly nail. Besides, you want your nails to look stunning when you show off your humongous wedding ring. Choose your manicurist and pedicurist with care. In some cases, they can do more harm than good.

Get Off That Couch!

Everybody, rich or not, prefers a partner with confidence. But how do you approach a man or woman with the right kind of confidence? Rich people generally decide within a minute or two whether they want to meet and talk to you. Help make that decision easy for them. The best approach I have found is to simply walk up to a wealthy person and say, "I saw you from a distance, and I wanted to meet you, but I'm late for a meeting. Can I get your phone number or email address so I can drop you a line? Maybe we can have lunch." Don't waver a minute, speak with confidence, and before you know it you'll be entering their contact information into your cell phone. This type of interaction is appealing to someone with money. It is actually refreshing to meet someone who isn't intimidated by them. In addition to confidence, it helps if you know how to use humor. If you can make them laugh, they will associate this pleasure with you.

What else do you need to know to hook up with the money? The most important thing is to be unique. Rich men and women can be approached ten times a day by someone who wants to meet them. By being different, you will go a long way toward forging a financially beneficial relationship. Create some mystery that will leave them wanting to know more about you—and don't be afraid to disagree with them. They are constantly surrounded by an army of staff and yes-people, so the idea that someone would have the confidence to voice a different opinion can intrigue someone with money.

Your millionaire-in-waiting is not going to descend from the clouds bearing gifts and wedding proposals. No one is going to knock down your door, scoop you up into his arms, and whisk you away to eternal bliss. The phone doesn't ring if no one knows your number. You have to put yourself out there and take some risks to meet the right people.

Another concept you need to grasp is that you don't have to have any special talents to gain tremendous wealth—although a few special talents in the bedroom never hurt anyone! Other than the lack of a gag reflex or the stamina of a bull, targeted natural gifts don't exist. The good news is that your lack of some natural skill is irrelevant; talent has nothing to do with greatness. You can make yourself into any number of things, and you can even make yourself great. Persistence, hard work, and determination are the only prerequisites to vast wealth.

By "talent" I do not mean intelligence, motivation, or personality traits. It's an innate ability to do some specific activity especially well. In virtually every field of endeavor, most people learn quickly at first, then more slowly, and then stop developing completely. Yet a few do improve for years and even decades, and go on to greatness. The same is true when searching for a financially independent spouse. The first major conclusion is that nobody gets rich without work—even if he or she is just looking to marry money.

There's no such thing as a free brunch. Even the most accomplished people need about ten years of hard work before becoming world-class. In fact, this pattern so well established researchers call it the ten-year rule. Wealth and luxury isn't handed to anyone; it requires a lot of hard work. But that isn't enough. I've seen plenty of people spend the better portion of their life digging for gold without any success. What's missing? The best people in any field are those who devote the most hours to learning their craft. This means they must practice.

Let's break down this idea. Your goal is to marry for money. Before you do anything else, you first have to identify the millionaires and billionaires in your area and learn their marital status. Then you'll have to study their businesses, hangouts, pets, charities, artists, music, and vacation spots. After you've learned their every move, likes, dislikes, and whereabouts for the majority of the time, you'll need to make an occasional appearance. This takes practice to appear confident and nonchalant, almost like you're breezing through your normal haunt instead of appearing as if you're a pretender—or worse, a stalker! But by continually observing results and making appropriate adjustments to your schedule, you become more confident and familiar with your surroundings and can focus on what you are there to achieve.

Consistency is vital. Through the whole process of searching for your lottery ticket, one of your goals is to build what the researchers call "mental models of your business," pictures of how the elements fit together and influence one another. The more you work on what you want your life to look and feel like, the larger your mental models will become and the better your performance will grow.

It's very much like an actor who performs a role for the first time. It feels awkward and unnatural at first. But by the hundredth performance, the actor has really become the character. This is similar to what happens to those trying to infiltrate the ranks of the wealthy. At first, they hang in the background and observe. But inevitably, by putting themselves into close proximity of wealthy people, they get to know a few. Next thing they know, they are being invited to go yachting with groups of wealthy friends or out to the summer house for a week. This exposes them to more wealthy people.

Eventually, you are able to look, walk, and talk as if you had billions, and it feels completely natural. This is when it happens—they perceive you as one of them and you become part of the "available" pool of people they would consider marrying.

Excuse Me, Which Way Is Rodeo Drive?

Now that we know what to do to attract a wealthy mogul, the biggest challenge is where to find one. Some of the venues for finding your money magnate are, of course, specific locations where the rich and famous hang out. It could be exclusive stores where the wealthy shop, nice restaurants where the wealthy dine, the first-class area of an airplane where the wealthy sit, and many more.

Meeting your sugar daddy or momma—whichever the case may be—has become a lot easier with the plethora of dating sites that cater to those who want to marry into money. The online dating phenomenon has enabled people to meet who otherwise would not cross paths. Many of these sites specialize in providing dating and matchmaking service to millionaires and people looking to marry millionaires.

Almost—if not totally—all of the millionaire dating service sites provide free membership for those looking for millionaires. But be careful; you never know who's lurking behind that screen name. There are some sites that do not verify authenticity of the member's income. Mr. or Ms. Moneybags could turn out to be bedridden and five hundred pounds, living off his or her mother's social security checks. To be on the safe side, you should look into the site's membership requirements. Some sites base the categorization on the member's good chance of becoming a millionaire in the near future and not on his or her current financial status.

Sites such as MillionaireMatch.com, SugarDaddie.com, and DateAMillionaire.com offer vast inventories of men and women who make the big bucks. Millionaire dating services work under the premise that millionaires, although they know what they want and need in a relationship, do not have the time to look for it. Of course they don't; when your time is worth more than 21,500 dollars per hour, you can't spend it trolling the bars for prospective mates. Thus, these sites aim to make the hunt easy. Millionaire dating sites provide technology such as chatting, emailing, and instant messaging used for online dating. Some offer a personalized matchmaking service.

Although most sites are free, some millionaire dating sites charge membership fees for millionaire members. These fees can be a bit hefty. But you need to look at the other services paid-membership sites offer, including personalized matchmaking, relationship coaching and counseling, style or fashion makeover, follow-up and feedbacks, and organized social events. If you live in the fast lane, opting for the add-on services could be very beneficial.

These sites have higher-profile members, such as CEOs, celebrities, and major sports figures, than broad-based sites such as Match.com and eHarmony. For example, actor Charlie Sheen was a member of MillionaireMatch.com for a few months.

In addition to millionaire dating sites, myriad other niche sites abound. In Beverly Hills, Spark Networks operates thirty special-interest dating sites, including the popular JDate.com for Jewish singles; there are also BlackSingles.com and ChristianMingle.com.

You can choose any category to date from, so why not choose a millionaire?

Another great way to snag an in to marrying a millionaire is to work for one. Executive assistants have a history of becoming the next Mr. or Mrs. in a millionaire's life. This type of job also allows you to combine your need for cash flow with your hunt for the perfect spouse. Even if your employer is taken, millionaires associate with other millionaires, so you have access to their contacts. When business associates drop by for an appointment, you have time to chat and get to know them on a one-to-one basis while their guard is down. Everyone chats with the secretary!

Don't think this is exclusive to women either. I know a female executive at a top bank who married a man from the accounting department at that same bank. He didn't work directly for her, he worked for the woman who worked for the guy who worked for her! But just the fact that they frequently ran into each other in the building and at company functions was enough for him to marry into the executive suite.

Stalking Your Prey

There is no end to the ways in which you can strategically place yourself so as to stumble across the rich and ultra-rich, but let's talk a few specifics: For example, the so-called Golden Triangle in Los Angeles holds more wealth and fine stores than most small countries. At its center is the renowned Rodeo Drive, the street on which Julia Roberts had her shopping spree in *Pretty Woman.* It is the street that sports designer stores such as Tiffany's, Cartier, Chanel, Bally, Gucci, and other well-heeled notables. On nearby Wilshire Boulevard, there is the Regent Beverly Wilshire, Niketown, Barneys, and yes, the notorious "Winona" Saks Fifth Avenue. And throughout the Triangle, you will see a curious collection of nouveau-riche types sauntering about; it will make you feel like you are watching an episode of "Lifestyles of the Rich and Famous."

You don't have to buy; window shopping *is* allowed. This is also true of luxury car dealerships. If you are a guy, looking for a car while you're looking for a mate is a good way to be of assistance to the wealthy woman who is wary of car dealers. You can "do lunch" at some of the nicest hotels and hot spots in Los Angeles for a song while rubbing elbows with the rich. Some industrious wealth seekers have been known to work as wait and hotel staff in upscale locations to learn how to spot the rich and to know them by name. Then when they show up at the occasional charity event, they seem to know everyone, and while they may look familiar to some, no one would imagine they used to be the "help." Remember the Jennifer Lopez movie, *Maid in Manhattan*? Her character was the perfect example of someone who saw the opportunity and took it—and ended up very wealthy indeed.

Another good area to seek out the whales is by traveling. Many people meet up on cruises and yacht tours, and if you get to know a good travel agent, he or she can find you super deals on the most exclusive vacations. No one needs to know you got your room free or at a huge discount.

Real estate is also a fabulous way to meet the person of your dreams. Whether through being a Realtor or just learning about real estate investment in the global market, you can catch the eye of many a millionaire. Most own real estate for investment purposes, and you will be able to share that interest.

Here again, it becomes a process of do what the rich do, think what the rich think, and go where the rich go. There is no limit to the ways and means, and these are only a few ideas to get your creative juices flowing.

Peek-a-Boo, I See You

Now that you have a basic idea of what you need to do, let's talk about focusing on the life you want to live and setting specific goals to get there. Everyone has a vision of how they would like their life to be. I find often that people get too caught up in the big picture to see the path they are supposed to follow. They get distracted with the mundane and lose focus on the target. We've all heard the phrase "seeing is believing." I disagree, because to me believing is seeing. Once you believe you can be rich, you will create that reality.

I once heard a self-help guru who looked like Moses say, "To think is to create." His point was if you think your life is crap and you think you are poor, you are. If you focus on your life being easy and living in wealth, you will eventually create that reality. This is not about fantasy. It's about focused intention. Concentrating on the bad in life just brings more of it to you. That's why we have clichés such as "misery loves company." Once you start whining about what you don't have, then so does everyone around you—and it escalates from there. You're depressed, your friends are depressed, your dog is depressed—and this is a choice. You can choose to wallow and roll around in your mental manure—or hose yourself off, leave the misery behind, and create a different existence.

Remember if you didn't have the right mindset about your right to be rich, then your life isn't going to change. The same is true with your vision: If you don't believe you can marry a millionaire—or billionaire for that matter—then it's not going to happen. Through the power of visualization, you can accomplish your goal of marrying for money. By actually seeing yourself standing at the altar in Italy next to your mogul in front of a star-studded crowd, you are able to achieve it more easily. In fact, by visualizing your dreams and acting as if you have already accomplished them, you'll be sauntering down the aisle before you know it.

Wear Your Wealth

This dream of marrying for money will only become a reality once you make it so in your mind. Don't believe me? Do me a favor; the next time you're standing in front of your closet wondering what to wear when you go out in search of your golden goose, don't just think about your clothes for that night. Instead, envision your life as a millionaire. Imagine standing in your 1,500-square-foot closet with ladders to reach the top shoe racks. But go even beyond that and think about your daily life: Imagine cruising the Mediterranean with a glass of wine while you deepen your tan. Smell the salt spray and listen to the lilt of sexy Italian staff members at your service. Then imagine jetting back over in your Gulfstream 4 to attend the Kentucky Derby in a private box.

Whatever you want in this new lifestyle, think about already having it. Imagine it in exquisite detail. Once you begin to envision yourself in those situations ask yourself these questions: *How would I walk? How would I talk? How would I think? Would I be witty or wobbly?* Wear your wealth from the inside out; become that person now. It takes practice. You will feel embarrassed at first—especially in front of your current friends—but so what? As a matter of fact, you should dump most of those losers anyway.

Look at your list of current friends. Ask yourself if those are the people you really want to be around, then take the appropriate actions. Get rid of the whiners, complainers, crybabies, or no-action dreamers. Keep and search out the ones who uplift you, support you, and treasure you. Keep the few who care enough to be authentic with you through good or bad times.

The key is to see it first and make it happen now. This visualization will allow your mind to start working on solutions even while you go on to other things. Just like you often have epiphanies in the shower when your mind is relaxed, putting these specific intentions in your subconscious mind will allow it to search for solutions and then *bam!* It will suddenly hit you what the obvious next step is.

In any undertaking of this magnitude, it is essential to set both long- and short-term goals. For a goal to be effective it must be very specific and have a distinct time frame. It must also be achievable—not fantasy as in "I'm going to be Tom Cruise's love slave."

Long-term goals include the type of millionaire you want to marry, from what geographic area, and in what time frame. Short-term goals should include getting a different job and researching the local millionaire scene. Short-term goals should also include an exercise program. If you truly want to marry into money, you've got to drop the flab and replace lethargy with vitality. Other short-term goals might include reaching your ideal weight (however you get there), a trip to a high-end hair stylist, and if money allows it, a weekly massage and spa treatment.

Let's take an example.

Macy is a twenty-nine-year old corporate secretary in Hoboken, New Jersey. She decides she wants to marry someone with at least 20 million dollars and live part of the year in Italy. Her goal sheet looks like this:

Long-Term Goals

1. Marry a millionaire worth at least 20 million dollars within five years.

2. Live six months each year in an Italian villa on the Mediterranean.

Short-Term Goals

1. *Get a job at an art gallery in the city that specializes in Italian art within the next month.* This will expose Macy to the international jet set that is specifically interested in Italian art. Your perfect match doesn't have to hail from New York or Los Angeles—or even from the States. Italy, England, and other locations have millionaires who might fit the bill and who would love to marry an American.

2. *Learn Italian and the Italian countryside like a local.* Being knowledgeable about where you eventually want to live makes you interesting as a person and gives you a great topic to discuss with the millionaires with whom you come into contact. You can read books, take classes, watch travel shows, and talk to anyone you know who is from Italy. Go down to Little Italy in New York and get to know people who can teach you the ins and outs. If at all possible, you should also visit the country, but if finances are prohibitive, then at least learn the area, the people, the history and the customs so intimately it will almost seem as if you've been there.

3. *Upgrade my wardrobe over the next months.* This may take a little while to do, but Italy is known for its fashion and millionaires will expect that you dress the part.

You can apply these goal-setting principles anywhere from California to Houston to South Carolina. The emphasis is on setting goals you can achieve that move you forward in your quest, and doing something positive and measurable to reach them.

Going for the Gold

Your prey is not going to ask you to marry him just because you want him to. For the record, the 1950s are long gone, and no one is going to marry you because of an "accidental" pregnancy either. And for all you young men who are poking holes in your condoms as we speak, woman no longer get embarrassed by a big stomach and a naked left finger, so don't think your millionaire sugar momma needs you for anything other than a sperm donation.

The only way you're going to hook your Orca is if he or she has strong and compelling reasons for wanting it to happen. If you want this person, you have to show why it is in his or her best interest to marry you. Single, rich individuals are available everywhere, but suitable partners can be hard to come by for the jet set. It will simply be a matter of how well you play your cards.

For anyone to be successful in their goal to marry for money, you must be ever vigilant of the various ways and means to get noticed. You must be able to draw attention to yourself in a positive way and create a lasting impression at the same time. The wealthy have a tendency to feel superior, so they will likely be attracted by what they perceive to be the best, the smartest, or the prettiest.

And notice I didn't say all that has to come in the same package. The trend these days is brains over beauty, so that

MBA could be worth substantially more than a pretty face—although they both have value. The person who not only catches a wealthy person's attention but has the ability to hold it through conversation creates a lasting impression that may win the key to his or her heart—and vault.

In your quest for capital, however, don't make the common mistake of focusing on yourself or coming across like a participant on "American Idol." The wealthy don't really care about what you had for dinner last night, your favorite movie, or how many times you go to the gym during the week. Quite honestly, they don't even care about what you want. How do you think the mega-rich amassed their millions? Certainly not by wondering how many times you go to the gym. Nope, my friend, it's all about them. Wealthy people are used to doing what they want when they want. They expect you to be interesting and interested in them—so learn the art of asking questions, then let them ramble. An obligatory nod or "Oh, really" is all it takes for them to feel as if you are the best conversationalist on the planet. If they are excited about what they are telling you, you are doing well.

It shouldn't be a surprise to learn that most millionaires are interested only in doing what they want to do and what is in their best interest to do. Your job is to prove that marrying you will be to their benefit in some way. This is a never-ending process—even after you've tied the knot. Remember, they can dump you any time they decide you no longer fit into their lives. Concentrate on being an asset. Make all of their needs your utmost priority. Don't worry, though; bide your time listening to them regale about their feats because once you have a ring on your finger, you'll soon pouring out your own life story to bored people who will nod and cater to *your* every whim.

One note of caution: No amount of money can make up for the fact that a person is whacked. As you move further along in your relationship, you need to determine whether or not he or she is crazy or has some strange sexual preferences. A Mercedes doesn't make up for hot buttered rum in your butt and shackles around your ankles—well, unless you too are into that sort of thing. The fact that people with money can have anything means some of them are what others politely call "eccentric," which for most of us means "perverse and weird." Just be ready to run if you find out your target is a more than a little off.

Getting to know your target can mean many different things, so as your relationship develops you should step up your knowledge on subjects that interest him or her. If, for example, you meet someone whose family business is publishing, you might want to take a few trips to the library and brush up on your reading. If you meet someone who is passionate about golf, take a few lessons and hit the course. Spend time with this person doing what he or she wants to do. Remember, this may be tedious now, but when you're in the money, you can do whatever you want.

Once you pass the six-month mark in a relationship, realize this person has invested a significant amount of time with you, so use this to your advantage. It's obvious he or she thinks highly of you or this person would not be spending valuable time with you; consequently, now is the time to find his or her Achilles heel. Everyone has weaknesses; we just don't like to admit them. Money doesn't exclude you from flaws, so even millionaires have things they don't want just anyone to see. But when you find a soft spot, help him or her hide it. You'll increase your value to by becoming a complementary partner.

Do anything you can to help in areas where he or she is lacking. If someone lacks the ability to remember names, for instance, work on your own memory. This is an invaluable tool when the two of you are at a social function. Saving him or her from embarrassment by whispering someone's name just before the introduction increases your net worth tenfold. Look for any way you can balance their skill—or lack thereof.

You may be thinking to yourself, well this sounds great, but don't the rich have personal assistants or secretaries for this? Yes, they do; but this is *your* financial future we're talking about. Rich people can't be seen hobnobbing with their wealthy associates with a paid employee on their arm. All these tasks are opportunities for you to add value by being helpful and by also making them look as if they are involved with someone. Even rich people don't like to show up stag to events. Your help weaves you deeper into his or her life, integrating your lives until they become almost seamless.

Summary

- ☾ The lifestyle of the wealthy takes an immense amount of cash.
- ☾ Marrying the jet set is not out of reach if you have the right mindset.
- ☾ Your happiness outweighs anyone else's opinion.
- ☾ Wear your wealth from the inside-out.
- ☾ You must be unique to make an impression; a little mystery goes a long way.
- ☾ Millionaires are not difficult to meet; you just have to know their habits.
- ☾ You must set goals to get what you want.

Four: My Butler Can Beat Up Your Butler

It is not the strongest of the species that survive, nor the most intelligent, but the one most responsive to change.
—*Charles Darwin*

IN ORDER TO MAKE IT TO THE NUPTIALS and the honeymoon on the beach, and out of your low-rent apartment to the mansion, you have to assimilate into the wealthy lifestyle as quickly as possible. You are now one of "them," so your old ways are no longer acceptable. If you want to fit into your new way of life, you have to think, act, and handle money like the wealthy.

The inner circle of the wealthy is comparable to a small town. Everyone knows everyone and they all talk. Since you are now the latest country club gossip, you need to be aware of the appropriate ways to handle yourself and act like a born and bred blueblood instead of a wannabe. You can't allow yourself to get frustrated in a social situation, lose your composure, and make a stupid remark such as, "Oh yeah? Well, my butler can beat up your butler." This only makes you look like new money—which in their eyes is a mortal sin—and shames the family of your wealthy meal ticket. There are certain ways the rich live that separate them from everyone else.

Becoming wealthy overnight is a dream come true—until the weight of responsibility sinks in. A life unaccustomed to great wealth goes through a number of transitions during the adjustment period, including:

("Money shock" when your own identity is being re-evaluated
(Guilt or unease about acquiring sudden wealth
(Pressure from family, friends, charitable organizations, and others who want to "share" your new affluent lifestyle
(Concerns about maintaining the money for yourself and your children
(Difficulty making informed decisions
(Lack of sufficient knowledge about how to manage the money and hesitance in admitting it
(Challenges in finding friends with similar means or difficulty trusting new relationships

Is There a Doctor in the House?

Affluenza became a recognized condition in the nineties because of the increased numbers of people coming into large amounts of wealth. This is also known as "sudden wealth syndrome." What exactly is affluenza? It is a dysfunctional or unbalanced relationship with money that manifests itself in a number of ways , and it is not just confined to the binge behavior of popular stereotype where you end up with a ridiculous grill on your teeth and ten-pound chain around your neck. With this sudden windfall, you may experience feelings of shame, guilt, anger, fear, rampant materialism, and hoarding. Some experience panic attacks, severe depression, and insomnia. Still others withdraw from society or go on maniacal shopping sprees. Often, these newly rich feel guilty about having so much money and believe they are not entitled to it or do not deserve it. Others become paranoid, thinking they will be exploited because of their wealth, or they become obsessed with making even more money.

People most affected are the "new rich," those for whom wealth was not part of their upbringing and who expected to spend their lives working. These are all symptoms of the condition. Affluenza or sudden wealth syndrome may seem like a made-up problem or disease, but the fact is that stress comes from change, and even a positive turning point such as becoming rich can be difficult to handle. The reality is that it's just a different host of issues that come with sudden wealth, as comes with any rite of passage such as childbirth or marriage or death or taxes. It's actually similar to symptoms that people experience during any major change in their lives. There's the shock period. There's the questioning period. There's the lack of trust—as in, "Is this for real?"

Feel the Force, Be the Force

There is a vast difference between dating a millionaire and being a millionaire. When you sit and twist your hair at your secretary desk daydreaming or scribbling on a sticky note about your new lavish lifestyle, you probably think all this money would be easy to handle. Finally, after all the drudgery and crap you have had put up with, you could have whatever you want. Sudden wealth syndrome never even entered your mind and almost seems like a ridiculous fabricated problem for a hypochondriac (okay, a rich hypochondriac). It almost seems like something called affluenza should be cured with a quick penicillin shot, no problem.

For far too many people, however, it doesn't work that way. Unlike those born into money and raised with it, those new to it don't know how to handle it. And one or two little surprises can highlight the fact that you don't blend in with your new crowd. For example, I was in a primo restaurant on an exclusive cruise ship recently and seated next to me was an older gentleman with a nice little piece of eye candy next to him—I would guess in her mid-twenties. They were joined by another couple about his same age, obviously friends or business associates. When the waiter took their order, the hot little number asked, "So what is 'pan searing'?"

Anyone who has progressed beyond Chicken McNuggets should know how to read a menu and what the basic definitions of cooking terms are. The raised brows on the couple across from them made it clear they did not (and probably will not) consider her one of them. First impressions are lasting and you can be certain this little faux pas was probably shared—and laughed about—with all his friends and family the minute the ship docked.

The rich will often test you to see if you are shaken by their abundant display of wealth. They will talk about Swarovski chandeliers, and they will see if you know the difference between a valet and a butler. Even if your beloved doesn't, his family and friends will. You may be quizzed on classes of yachts, various ul-tra-exclusive resorts for quick getaways, and even private boarding schools (And you thought those were a thing of the past!).

> One of the items that can really rattle someone new to money is the amount and number of support staff necessary to run multiple mansions.

One of the items that can really rattle someone new to money is the amount and number of support staff nec-essary to run multiple mansions. You may think it's not much differently that your life now except that the yard gets mowed, house cleaned and cooking done by someone else—but its much more than that. There are numerous staff members including one (or two) drivers, pilots, housekeeping, and dining service workers. This could include as many as twenty people in your house besides you at any one time in the house to keep things running. Keep this in mind if you want to run down to the fridge in the buff for a late night snack. You don't want Hazel counting your pubes while they are illuminated by the fridge light.

You Must Exorcise Your Mother

No, I don't mean take the old bag to a spinning class—that's exorcise not exercise! All of us—even those raised in a tenement on wheels—had certain things drilled into our brains as children. Things such as:

℃   Pick your clothes up off the floor
℃   Make your bed
℃   Put your dishes in the sink
℃   Feed the dog
℃   Keep your shoes out of the living room
℃   Don't put your wet towels on the floor

These are the things that will trip you up in the world of the rich. They don't do their own laundry, clean their own rooms, or feed their own pets; they have people for that. The interesting thing is that these activities were instilled into our minds and are such a habit, you may do them without even thinking and thus reveal your poseur status. No matter how silly it may seem to you for someone to make your bed or help with trivial items, you must allow the staff to do their jobs and go on as if it is the expected way of things. You can't freak out if they help you with your bags or your coat or put a napkin in your lap—just roll with it.

No matter how extensively you plan and train yourself, there will be some occasions that leave you completely stumped as to how to respond. You may suddenly find yourself at a party with a Japanese theme and plates full of squiggly things that resemble half-eaten bait. Not only will you have no clue what they are, but you also may not want to risk puking on the host if one of those squiggly parts goes down wrong. In this situation, your best bet is to watch what others are eating the most of and how they go about it. Odds are that selection will be the most palatable and you can observe the correct technique before you attempt it just in case the morsel is hotter than habanero Cheese Whiz.

There may also be formal occasions where you are seated with a place setting consisting of more silverware than your parents ever owned. Again, observe those around you and work the utensils from the outside in. That's not to say you will be adept at using said utensils. Anyone who remembers the snail-eating scene from the movie *Pretty Woman* knows there are indeed "slippery little suckers" and sometimes you will just blow it. When it happens, just keep your sense of humor and keep right on going. If you are absolutely too intimidated to try some of the offerings, don't despair. There is always a burger joint on the way home that will allow you to supersize.

As far as fashion mistakes, the red carpet is full of them these days. Outrageous fashion in the millionaire strata screams, "Look at me! I'm insecure with my wealth and need attention!" While this may seem a good idea to attract the attention of a mate, it is really the opposite. You want to blend with the bluebloods, not have them ask the staff to watch your every move. So remember—classic looks are the best.

An ascent into the real world of wealth is much like a political campaign. You aim for your target but you must also rally support within his or her camp. You must convince those around your millionaire that you are a great catch, thereby lessening the potential opposition. If you choose outrageous ways to stick out, they will encourage Mr. or Ms. Moneybags to keep you as "fling" material rather than spouse material.

Marketing Yourself to Maximum Advantage

I have built my career on teaching people how to market their business or product. This includes pointing out the possible pitfalls and how to avoid them. Several years ago I wrote a book called *The 10-Minute Marketer's Secret Formula*. The whole point of this book was to teach businesspeople how to get others interested in their product using nontraditional means. Rather than taking out a billboard to show your wares, you get people talking. When I thought of the idea for the book you now hold in your hands, it was based on the same concept—except the product you are marketing is you as opposed to widgets.

There are specific steps to take when pursuing someone in the millionaire strata of the population, and once you identify this as your target market, you simply concentrate your efforts to making the most of what you have.

The first step is to build on your strengths. If you volunteer and do community work, then try and be a spokesperson for the organization. Get your face on the news and in the paper for doing good. Rich and poor alike read the paper, and even if you flip burgers on the side, the fact that you are well known and liked by the public can be an attractive asset for your future benefactor.

> Marketing yourself is not about the big score. It is small victories of acceptance until you reach that inner circle.

One of the mistakes I often see gold-diggers (Oops! I mean "financial ascenders.") make is that they try to hit one out of the park on the first swing. Marketing yourself is not about the big score. It is small victories of acceptance until you reach that inner circle. It's grinding it out attending galas, charity events, and auctions. It's educating yourself by watching the Travel Channel and perusing a cooking terms encyclopedia. To be that one-in-a-million who married a million, you have to set goals and objectives and consistently work toward them.

This doesn't mean you just jump in anywhere. You don't want to embarrass yourself right off. It is important to sit back and develop a marketing strategy rather than start showing up at the ball like a Trojan-crazed Cinderella. You want to identify the players and work your way to the people who can do you the most good in promoting yourself. Those who will talk you up to the single billionaires they come across. You are just one person, so don't spread yourself too thin. Leveraging these other contacts gives you more exposure than you might gain yourself.

As you implement your plan, you must also measure progress. I know this seems a little odd to track how close to the altar you come every day, but it is necessary. It will encourage you and keep you on course so it is less likely you will quit. It is also important to use this information to evaluate your results. Are you getting any response or not with certain actions? Or are you getting the wrong types of response? A few years ago, I met a woman in her late thirties named Beth. Beth was convinced the only males she attracted were short, bald Mexican men with no pesos. After a few weeks and stories of her escapades in the dating world, it seemed she was right. Although she was attractive and outgoing, the only men who asked her out were short, bald Mexican men who wanted her to pay for their tequila. This was a perfect opportunity to evaluate where Beth was going wrong in her approach.

We chatted over coffee, and I quickly realized from our conversation that Beth had fallen into some of her old habits without even realizing it. She'd gone back to interacting with old friends and family instead of sticking to her new wealthy existence. Interestingly enough, Beth didn't even realize she'd done it, which is why analyzing where you are and how far you have come are so important. It will allow you to highlight issues like Beth had and do away with them before they interfere with your progress.

Pace Yourself

One of the worst things you can do is to assume after a short time (or a one-night stand) that you and your millionaire are a done deal. While it's great to be excited and think positively, that doesn't mean you should trade the Honda for a Hummer quite yet. You have to hold off and see how things go, or you could completely undermine all your hard work.

> One of the worst things you can do is to assume after a short time (or a one-night stand) that you and your millionaire are a done deal.

After you start dating the rich, one of the first problems you will be faced with is the interference of friends and family, some of whom will undoubtedly think that if you're sleeping with a rich person, their money will rub off on you. So don't be surprised if relatives start hitting you up for cash. Although this may be largely your own doing as you chatter on about your mark's money, these friends and relatives may invite themselves along on shopping sprees, hoping to catch a few crumbs from your gravy train. They live by the motto, "A score for you is a score for the family." Well, that is not exactly true. The change in your status can occur so quickly you just don't have time to adjust to their behavior—nor they to yours.

This is a heart-wrenching dilemma because although you don't want to turn your back on your family, you can't afford to bank roll them either. Carefully examine the need that is being presented to you. Choose which people you consider to be in your innermost circle. Budget some percentage of your windfall to help family members and friends who are truly in need, and stick to the budget so your own goals do not get subverted by the troubles of loved ones. Family issues are complicated and multilayered and can potentially ruin your millionaire marriage.

Your relatives don't know how to be rich any better than you do, so expect them to look like hillbillies. Knowing this, you should put off that first meeting with your intended as looooooong as you can—for both your sake and theirs.

The 64,000-dollar question—or in this case the 64-million-dollar question—is how can you adapt into this lifestyle? You know there must be some connection between money and happiness. If there weren't, you wouldn't have spent the last six months to a year plotting your every move to meet a millionaire. The relationship between money and happiness, it would appear, is more complicated than the Excel spreadsheets you used to stalk your spouse.

This new, ultra-wealthy lifestyle can and will bring you eternal happiness as long as you know just what you can and can't expect from it.

Real life is never as good as your dreams; more than likely you've overestimated how much pleasure you'll get from having millions of dollars. And soon you'll see that the millionaire or billionaire you put on a pedestal is actually human just like the rest of us. Yes, this money makes you happy in the short-term, and it absolutely makes life much easier, but you will quickly adjust to your new wealth—and everything it buys you.

If you do strike it rich, the best advice is to take some time and just breathe. Give yourself plenty of time to think about what you really want to do. Remember that money gives you the freedom to be you—only bigger.

Let's say you have hooked up with Mr. or Ms. Maybe and things are progressing well. Now your lover hands over come cash or plastic to use at your discretion. I'll warn you that this could also be a trick for him or her to see how you handle it. This sudden influx of money brings with it a kind of adrenaline rush and can push you into a kind of spending frenzy. Don't act like a drunken sailor in a whore house. Instead make sure to purchase wisely and with an eye to how your intended might feel about those purchases. Do you want to overspend now and risk losing your cash cow, or do you want to be conservative (yet grateful) and plan for the big score at the altar?

You don't have to live out your vision of how a rich person lives. More than likely, while you were sweltering in front of a swamp cooler in your ghetto apartment, your delusions of the grand life were based on Hollywood. This is real life not the movies. Discern between needs and wants. Don't look across the lawn at your neighbor's pool house and think "I want one too." Separate your emotions from your money and don't base your happiness on the bank balance. Instead, find hobbies or activities that nourish you and not your ego. Most wealthy people don't go on humongous spending sprees every week (How else do you think they keep their money?). Books such as *The Millionaire Next Door* reveal that truly wealthy people live well beneath their means, investing for their future rather than living flamboyantly.

When you marry into money, you are not used to such riches. This can eventually result in feelings either of guilt or of worthlessness, with no direction or purpose in life other than to spend all that money.

But you think you can handle it, don't you? But are you prepared? Would you know what to do if you did marry all these millions? One day to have relatively nothing, the next to have several millions? Would you go the same way? Of course, you would. My fundamental advice to anyone who marries into money is to greet the transition as they do other major life changes. Be patient and don't underestimate the magnitude of the opportunities and challenges but realize that acclimatization can take a while.

Summary

(Know the signs of sudden wealth syndrome.

(Don't get rattled by a significant display of wealth.

(Get your mother's advice out of your head.

(If you don't know how to act in a particular instance, watch others.

(Marketing yourself requires discipline.

(Have patience with family as they might not adjust to wealth as quickly.

Five: Show Me the Monet!

"Money can't buy love, but it improves your bargaining position."—*Christopher Marlowe*

THERE ARE MANY SCAM ARTISTS IN THE world today, and money is usually at the root of these slimeballs' motives. Documents can be forged with today's technology, and a fake Rolex looks no different than a real one. Before wasting valuable time, you need to understand the various methods to ensure you're dealing with an honest-to-goodness millionaire or billionaire. Nothing could be worse than uttering the words "I do" only to find out on your wedding night that your "millionaire" is the assistant manager at the local Slurp and Burp.

A good example of this made the headlines in September 2008. A man who called himself Clark Rockefeller intimated he was related to the actual Rockefellers, but in reality he was a German citizen who was not connected to the Rockefellers—or to their money. A minimal investigation of his background would have divulged the falsehood to his wife of seven years, but she took him at his word and didn't learn the truth until he kidnapped their daughter after their divorce. Don't make this mistake! People will embellish or even downplay their wealth depending on their own self-interests, so you must verify as much as you can.

How exactly do you broach this awkward conversation? You don't. There are numerous ways to check someone out without demanding information. It is important to do this research as quickly as possible and to check out any additional tidbits of details as the relationship progresses. The last thing you want to do is get hooked up with someone whose family is wealthy but he or she is penniless.

How to Spot a Lemon

Being wealthy and acting rich are very different things. One of those things involves having money—lots of it. The other of those things involves saying you have money—and lots of it. Finding a high net-worth husband or wife has nothing to do with luck and everything to do with applying good research and investigative skills. Knowing how to spot potential problems and determining how much money they really have can save you from many headaches down the road. You want to make certain that your millionaire is who you assume he or she is, and that he or she meets your income and asset requirements. This being said, you can't exactly walk up to a lady getting into her limo and ask her out for a cup of coffee with the condition that she bring her financial statement—unless you want a Prada stiletto stuck up your butt.

People who act as though they are rich, but who are in reality wealthy wannabes, give themselves away by making their lives sound more important than they are. You know the drill. They brag about the country club, the home on the hill, and the private plane. What they don't tell you is that their club dues are in arrears, the home is mortgaged to the hilt, and the private plane is a used Cessna on life support. They are often boisterous, loud, and hungry. A restaurant is the best place to see this circus in action. There is a magnificent mix of people from the entire trailer park feasting on everything and anything. They constantly remind the wait staff how well they tip and spout out for all to hear about how much money they make.

Wannabes use the phrase "poor folk." Actually, they refer to everyone as "folk." Stop and think about this for a moment:

Have you ever heard Donald Trump call the contestants on "The Apprentice" folks? Imagine the last five minutes of the show; he sits down at the table with them, straightens his comb-over, and says, "Folks, tonight one of you is going home." Social climbers always name drop and talk about any famous or important people. Really, you don't even need to have traveled to California for this. Just pick a washed-up celebrity people don't remember anymore.

The tawdry fashion sense—not to mention the brash and tasteless manners they exhibit—is a dead giveaway. You know who they are and what they do. They enter a room and suddenly they start talking about where they came from and what they bought. I actually once overheard a woman who said, "I just arrived from Europe, and you know when I come home from Europe, I have to buy extra luggage because of all the expensive trinkets I buy when I am there." That is tacky. And pathetic. But it is true and it is common.

The wannabe rich are arrogant and pathetic but a great source of entertainment.

Your Past Can Come Back to Bite You

Let me caution you that while you may be checking out the wealthy, they may also be scrutinizing you. Activities that seem fun at the time can have some nasty consequences. With the advent of the Internet, what happens in Vegas doesn't always stay in Vegas. YouTube, for example, has opened the doors to millions of content creators eager to say, do, and broadcast something—anything—to whoever will listen or watch.

In addition to paving the way for the unheard masses, YouTube enables us to record, play, and rewind the events in which we participate. It also enables others to share our experiences with the entire globe and make them even more meaningful and interesting. What we cannot see, however, in a three-minute YouTube video are contexts, circumstances, and trajectories of events. And yet on the basis of a three-minute video, people's lives have been ruined and reputations destroyed. No amount of apologies or explanations can undo a video posted on the Internet.

On a side note: No matter how much you think you're in love, never ever get out the camera. A picture is worth a thousand words and in some cases that pictures could cost you millions of dollars.

Facebook, one of the world's most used and talked about websites, is at the center of a debate about social networking that has perplexed millions of us. What is really on display on these sites? Is it business networking or some titillating trek into the sexual side of attraction? Amy Polumbo, Miss New Jersey 2007, is a prime example of the dangers of sites such as these. She didn't lose her crown, but many believe she lost a good-standing reputation because of content posted that showed her as a sex kitten.

If you are in the public eye, you shouldn't be taking pictures that are the least bit questionable and posting them on Facebook or anywhere else. And believe it or not, the fact that the photos were more ridiculous than anything is what brought down Amy's credibility as a decent state beauty pageant representative. Jealous friends and suspicious relatives will do what it takes to dig up dirt. This includes posting that Lil' Abner musical you sang in as a high school sophomore and that big hair you sported in the late eighties.

Almost every cell phone has a camera these days, and some are so discreet they are virtually undetectable. If you and your girlfriends went to New Orleans for spring break, and you decided to flash your goods for a stack of beads, don't be too surprised if you're not the latest feature on some social networking site. Or if you're the type of guy who screws every girl you meet, ransacks her wallet, and shimmies down the drain pipe before she wakes up, more than likely you'll be the subject of a viral email by an angry not to mention broke one-night-stander.

Don't think for a minute that Daddy Warbucks isn't going to search every nook and cranny of your life before he lets you into the family. If you stripped your way through college only to move five states away to hide your past, it's not going to work. That pole will follow you for the rest of your life. Before you walk in the door to meet the parents, they'll already know your past relationships, family history, and underwear size. Also, if your past is less than angelic, you may be approached by dirty ole Uncle Joseph. He knows you gave it up to the masses in the past, so why wouldn't he try to get a piece of the action?

So if you've got a checkered past, and you're thinking about hedging your bets and going for the family member with the most money, think again. Regardless of how good you are in bed, blood is thicker than water. Your potential in-laws are well acquainted with Google, and if any of your past can tarnish their reputation, you and your knockoff designer luggage will be on the front lawn before your crocodile tears dry.

Getting to Know You

The first step in getting to know your millionaire is to snag a business card. This usually provides a wealth of information. Job title gives you an idea of income level if he or she is a corporate executive. For example, if she is a director of a large oil company, you will be able to search wage comparison data for your area to get a good idea of what someone in that industry with that title makes. The U.S. government is a big help as well. The Bureau of Labor Statistics is a wealth of information as far as average salaries for certain positions.

If your target is a CEO or top executive, and the company is public, you get even more information. Each company must disclose the compensation they give their most senior executives. Even data a year or two old will give you a ballpark idea. Let's say you meet a guy in a bar in Texas, and he says he works for Exxon. You've heard through the grapevine that he does not make a million per year. He gives you a card that says he is a senior vice president and director. Google "executive pay disclosure" and choose a website sponsored by the Securities and Exchange Commission that lists executive pay disclosures. This allows you to choose a company or industry. Type in Exxon and receive a list of executive pay in 2006. Even if the names have changed from then to now, the pay will remain similar with cost of living adjustments.

I did this, and I found that the senior vice president and director at Exxon earned 935,000 dollars in 2006. Not bad. Even more interesting is that he received a bonus of 2.1 million dollars! He also received 3.2 million dollars in stock and a 2-million-dollar increase in pension. Along with other compensation, that is a whopping 8.58 million dollars in one year. So while it's true he doesn't make a million dollars in annual salary, there are more assets there than meet the eye.

Conversely, you may meet someone who says he or she earns a million dollars per year, After some digging, you find out that in reality much of that income is in the form of deferred compensation and perks, and this person really brings home much less.

A short bit of sleuthing can also uncover where your focus lives. Often, wealthy people are reluctant to give out their addresses, but if you know the general area, you can check county tax records online to not only find the address but the value of the home. You can also use county records to check on marriage documents, divorce documents, and other legal actions in which he or she may have been involved.

As you are searching the address, you may often uncover other useful information on family members or events such as weddings and obituaries. If your local paper has a society column, that can also be a useful source of information to learn who knows who and what connection they have to one another. Warning: Do-it-yourself detective work can be potentially fatal. One woman hid under her prey's SUV parked at a nightclub. She fell asleep and unfortunately, someone let all the air of the wheels out and trapped the poor woman under the car. When AAA arrived, the tow truck driver was shocked to discover a woman begging to get out from under that SUV! Can you say awkward?

Background checks are a great way to get this type of information. Once these were only performed by police and military personnel or other government offices, but they are now available to everyone from employers to apartment rental companies to schools. Individuals can use them too. Doing so will not only allow you access to criminal records and history with the law, but can serve to add to their credibility and standing in the community as well.

If you are pursuing multiple millionaires, you may not have time to do your own investigating. In this case, I recommend hiring a private investigator. Private investigators have become a well-integrated part of American culture, and most states require that they be licensed. The state of California, for example, makes sure that its private investigators pass a series of tests, are over the age of eighteen, have a police science background, pass a criminal background check, pass the requirements for a firearm permit, and cannot be a felon. For all you gold-diggers in the sun-kissed state, you'll be pleased to know that California has one of the most stringent standards for private investigators and is one of the best places to hire an investigator because of these standards.

Suspicion of adultery comes to mind as a good reason many people think about hiring a private detective. What most people don't realize is they're just as valuable before the relationship begins. These private investigators, who are sometimes ex-police officers or individuals who have some other law enforcement experience, are a fabulous resource as you gather supportive evidence of your target's millionaire status. It can, however, be expensive. And make sure you stash his or her business card in a safe place as you do not want your intended to find it.

Lucky for you, some of the resources that used to be available only to private investigators are accessible to you via the Internet. A good example of this is the reverse phone number search. All you have to do is go to a reverse trace number website and input the phone number you want more information on, and basic information such as number location will be displayed. If you want detailed information such as the phone number's registered owner and current address, address history, and even family members of that number, then all you have to do is join its yearly membership. For less than 40 bucks you can reverse search as many phone numbers as you like for an entire year. This is much more cost-effective and discreet than hiring a private investigator.

And here's another hint just for the guys: Listen to all that chick chatter! People talk about people in every social circle. You will learn a great deal about who owns what, who was married to whom, and which assets went with which spouse—and you don't even have to do anything but look interested and nod. Other wealthy people who chatter about their counterparts are wonderful sources of information and dirt. Think of it like insider trading: If you know something the populous at large doesn't, it gives you a huge advantage.

One problem with getting the scoop on assets from others is that it doesn't tell you how heavily leveraged those fabulous assets are. You are after those individuals with a high *net* worth—not someone with loans on everything they own. That home in Palm Beach may be worth 15 million but the owner could have a 14-million-dollar—or more—mortgage. That's one heck of a house payment! With the recent mortgage crisis, some may actually owe millions more than their house is worth. There are scores of people living large but may well be spending everything they earn—and more. Although they may make a tremendous amount of money, if more goes out than comes in, you're screwed—and not in a good way.

How many athletes and celebrities have you heard of who amassed huge fortunes only to be destitute ten to fifteen years later? It happens all the time. You want to be sure your millionaire isn't pulling the last of that home equity out of the castle to pay the electric bill. How do you find this information?

One of the easiest and best ways is to befriend a low-level teller or secretary at the financial institution where your millionaire does business. These people will often divulge information over drinks that would make their employers writhe in legal discomfort. With a click of the mouse, they will know by looking at personal accounts if there are large house payments, an ex-wife that is a significant cash drain, or if they are constantly overdrawn.

Those of you who doubt this approach have obviously never had a friend or family member who worked in a bank or brokerage. No matter how many privacy laws are passed, people are still people, and they talk—providing you with more information about your date's financial health than his or her mother even knows.

The Invisible Target

There are times when information is hard to come by—especially when you approach the upper strata of wealth. These people have spent years surrounding themselves with those who are loyal only to them and will never divulge information no matter how big the crowbar.

Those who are foreign and don't live permanently in the United States can also be difficult to find information on. In these instances, the blogs and social networking sites can really benefit you. Family members, exes, children, and employees can unintentionally—or intentionally—dish the dirt via a blog, Facebook, or MySpace. There are numerous social and business sites that will help you find people who know or travel in the same circles as those you want to know—even on the international scene.

In general terms, the more money someone has, the more difficult to get to them. Are there exceptions? Sure—Warren Buffet is notoriously easy to meet in person, especially if you frequent the coffee shops and diners of Omaha. But don't expect to get your hooks in him as he is definitely taken.

Scoping the Mansion

If you don't look, you usually won't find! In order to notice signs of a lying potential millionaire mate, you need to pay attention to what's going on in his or her life. There is nothing wrong with stepping back to look at this person from the outside to see if he or she is on the up and up. The problem with this, though, is that a lot of times you may notice things you normally overlook in the regular everyday routine.

One of these surprising things may be noticing the signs of a rich wannabe. These signs are usually only picked up by stepping back and observing or listening to your "spidy senses" or "gut feeling." We really do have a sixth sense, but it serves no purpose if we just ignore it when it is summoned.

Pay attention! Your boyfriend or girlfriend will leave signs and "evidence" behind. Write things down that don't make sense so you can refer back to them later. There is nothing wrong with asking a casual question requiring him or her to account for financial status. Make sure to keep it casual, though, and just simply record it (either mentally or by jotting it down later). Eventually, people will slip up on a follow-up question asked a day or two later.

One of the best ways to assess additional assets is to be invited into the personal kingdom. It can take literally months to gain entry through a relationship, so don't waste a minute of your time there and spend that time assessing the real value of those assets. To know what to look for and how to assess it, you must educate yourself. Although that painting over the sofa may be horrific to you, it could be a Picasso worth millions. The same is true of watches, clothing, jewelry, and cars.

What are the most exclusive handmade European cars? Which artists are the most popular among the younger rich crowd? What decorators do billionaires use? Who are their Realtors? If you are unfamiliar with the ultimate in high-end accessories, you must gather magazines and books, and teach yourself things only the ultra-rich know.

Interestingly enough, most of this information can be a challenge to find. This is because the rich usually value discretion, and therefore, few people will name them as clients or risk losing their business. However, once you start mingling at parties, this stuff makes great small talk. *Which designer did the host use for the pool house? What event planning company put on the benefit? Who is the best Realtor in Beverly?* Questions such as these seem benign, but once you know the answers, it is easier to blend in. Suddenly you will magically know the best yacht broker, the most popular up-and-coming architect, and the best law firm to handle those messy domestic hassles. Instead of being viewed as an outsider, you will have interesting information to share that makes you seem like one of them. And all the while they are sharing their secrets and skeletons.

Tempting as it may be to snoop through the mansion's home office to see what you can find, this is probably a huge mistake. There are numerous wealthy individuals who install cameras in sensitive areas of the home to prevent just such an invasion. Even the help may not realize they are being watched. Never snoop in drawers or desks as the risk of ruining your entire plan is just too high. The trust issue can't be underestimated and can't be regained once you are caught snooping.

One exception, in my opinion, is the master bath medicine cabinet. It's justified in my mind to know if your possible future spouse is doped up on lithium or has suicidal tendencies. It's also good to be aware if that hot and heavy sex was because he was bowled over by your charms—or because of a little blue pill. It can also reveal if your intended has any weird medical habits, such as fifty-seven different vitamins per day or pet leaches used for some bizarre cleansing ritual. And if you find a prescription for a sexually transmitted disease, take every precaution to get out of sex!

Other items to note are things that shouldn't be—such as women's cosmetics in his bath or an extra set of men's clothing in her closet. Is there evidence that the ex is still a frequent visitor for sleepovers? Do you get weird vibes from the staff?

Something else to note is whether the home is too sterile. This could indicate that the place is not their primary residence. On the surface, the house looks like it could have walked off the pages of a magazine, but cabinets and refrigerator are empty. No personal photos are displayed. In this case, he or she may have a home in the country and a penthouse in the city. This is one way wealthy married people have affairs and the mistress is blissfully unaware. Although many of the rich have second homes, they don't have residences that the family (or spouse) doesn't frequent. So if the house feels sterile, it probably is—on purpose. They don't want you to know they have family so they intentionally remove any hint of personal information or evidence.

Once you've scoped the house for clues, you should know a great deal about your target. The design they like, the hobbies they love, what family they treasure. These are great conversation starters to get them talking about the things they hold dear.

Family Album

Although it may sound odd, some of your best allies in landing the whopper may be the person's own family. Of course, Granny would love to see that boy settle down and have some babies, so she spouts a litany of helpful information about his past, his fears, and his hang-ups. And what about the thrice-divorced woman who inherited a fortune from her late husband? Well, you may find her sister's husband is more than a little tired of having the old bag's money constantly being pushed in his face. He can fill you in on the real family dirt and how much she is worth. The sister can even confide some lurid details as she is convinced the poor widow is slipping into a depression. You never know where the key tidbit of info will come from, but take what's offered and make yourself the perfect person to solve every issue your intended has.

This applies mostly to those who are self-made as they tend to have families who are not necessarily wealthy, and they may be less likely to guard the information closely. Bluebloods, however, are a different story. They've seen every money-making, social-climbing trick in the book—they invented them—so you must be much more low key. And be aware you are being watched. Although some of the family members gained entry just like you are planning to do, they are not about to let you hone in on their good deal. You will experience conniving, cheating, lying, and subversion in this situation, but still you must persevere.

You will know exactly how good you are by how hard they fight you. The more threatened they feel, the more vocally displeased they may be with the idea of you joining them. The good news is that if you are that good, you will win, and that is what they fear most. Once you are one of them, you might be able to get a better deal than they have. And nothing cuts to the quick of a gold-digger's heart than to be beat at his or her own game.

No matter the particular avenue you choose, family and friends can unwittingly help you in your quest. Even if the first try doesn't work out, all you learn and observe will help with contestant number two and before you know it you will walk, talk, and sound like a billionaire yourself.

A word of caution: If you are thinking of doing anything discussed above, prepare yourself for any potential consequences. Depending on the degree of your "investigating," you may violate criminal laws, civil codes, or common law. If you are going to use this proof of infidelity to blackmail or demean your partner and cause undue stress and trauma, you are liable to answer in court for your careless action.

If you can't risk your partner's ire and disgust, then don't snoop. Snooping often leads to distrust and the eventual dissolution of a relationship. Again, if you can't endure a breakup at this point, mind your own business.

Don't Boil the Bunny Rabbit

We've all seen the movie; Glenn Close goes nuts and boils Peter Cottontail. As screwed up as that sounds, horrific acts like that happen every day. Going beyond snooping is stalking, a crime in all fifty states. If you trail someone everyday and make mysterious calls to his workplace, you'll soon be clad in an orange jumpsuit. So when pursuing your money-honey, avoid these three deadly mistakes:

1. *Threatening behavior.* Any threat of violence against him or toward yourself will not only eliminate your chances of getting a date, but you may end up in court or jail. You may really want to get noticed, but threatening violence against her, a new guy in her life, or talking suicide is the worst mistake you can make.

2. *Crying and pleading.* Confidence is attractive. Crying and pleading is going to make him run away like you have the plague. Calling her up twenty times a day and begging for a date is more likely to creep her out than ever get you in the front door.

3. *Stalking.* Again, avoid the stalking! This includes following him, going past her house, and calling, texting, or emailing all the time—and all other behavior of this fashion. This type of persistent behavior frightens people.

Summary

(Be aware that anyone can fake anything these days.

(People will embellish or downplay based on their own self-interest.

(Know how to spot clues to potential problems or inconsistencies.

(The wealthy can and will check you out.

(Google your millionaire and see if there is information concerning his or her lifestyle in the article.

(The best inside information comes from other people.

Six: Planet Penis and the G-Spot Galaxy

If sex doesn't scare the cat, you're not doing it right.

—Anonymous

FOR THOSE OF YOU WHO RAN UPSTAIRS, pulled down the blinds, stripped down to your skivvies, and skipped ahead to this chapter in eager anticipation, I'm sorry to disappoint you, but there aren't going to be any pictures. Don't be too upset; you'll still stumble across an occasional naughty reference every now and again.

Let's face it; when it comes to sex men and women are as different as caviar and pimento cheese. The most obvious differences are below the belt (except for when silicone is involved), and many times we overlook the more important psychological differences. These differences are as old as the species itself and have been socially defined and distorted through a lens of sexism in which men assumed superiority over women and maintained it through emotional and physical domination because, well, if women ruled the world we might have things like world peace and frilly toilet lid covers. The psychological differences between the sexes are difficult to define and describe, yet they profoundly influence how we form and maintain relationships.

Adding the physical act of sex to the relationship equation further confuses everyone involved. I don't like to stereotype, and I'm sure I'm going to get some hate mail for this, but women tend to fantasize about sex on white satin sheets with candlelight and wine while men focus on quick and easy. The backseat or the couch in their buddy's apartment, clothes on or off, it doesn't matter; men for the most part just want to get laid.

Men don't sit around a martini bar and gab about how fulfilling their relationship is. As a matter of fact, most men don't even have the term "relationship" in their vocabulary. They instead may refer to a past relationship as "the time me and Christine were bangin' on the weekends." Beauty on the inside only matters if a guy is impotent.

Men are also notorious drunk dialers. After a night out at the bar, they might go home and call their ex, hinting for a midnight booty call. While they may insist she's a psycho witch from hell, after a few beers she's suddenly his best bet for a quickie.

Women, on the other hand, want to nurture their relationships. They use phrases like "taking it to the next level." Just a word of caution, and I think I speak for all guys, rich or poor, when I say this: There is nothing that will scare a man away as quickly as a woman with the wedding bell blues.

In college I had a good friend named Kyle, who took his prize cock (get your mind out of the gutter) Landry across state lines for the chicken fights. His girlfriend at the time, Megan, became increasingly irritated and disturbingly jealous of the amount of time he was spending with his chickens. (Yes, this is a true story, and no, my parents aren't brother and sister.) One evening as Kyle prepared to leave, Megan threw a fit and demanded he choose between her and the chickens. Needless to say, he chose his little feathered friends. True story. You see, men don't like ultimatums; we're self-centered and egotistical and along with our schlongs we need our egos stroked too.

Relationships today aren't difficult or impossible. Sadly, however, the society norm expects us to grow up, finish school, get married, have 2.3 kids, and live happily ever after. If you ask me, the end result is happily *never* after. These expectations are not only unrealistic but ultimately they leave people feeling unloved, inadequate, cynical, apathetic, or ashamed. This poses a problem for many who are looking for gold-plated love. Before you can venture out on your search, you've got to get rid of these false expectations. Stop trying to live according to what society wants. Go for what *you* want.

Is It Live or Is It Memorex?

Our sexual identity is central to who we are, and more so than ever we live in a sexualized culture as compared to earlier periods of repression and inhibition. In the 1950s and 1960s, the biggest dilemma on TV was which father knew best or how many mishaps Lucy and Ethel could get into. Could you imagine having a sitcom about a character named Beaver today? The FCC would be on that like white on rice!

Yet the media is full of sex. Sex, sex, and more sex. Unfortunately, television tends to glamorize sex. On any given channel, you'll invariably find a couple making love on the beach or kissing passionately as soon as they wake up. Both couples look beautiful, every hair in place, the sand is pristine, and the sheets are folded just so. In TV land maybe, but in the real world, sand gets in your butt and the stench of morning breath is enough to melt the paint off the walls. The visibility of sex in the media and its influence on how we understand sex is only thirty or forty years old.

Having sex with a person is no guarantee of a wedding ring. It doesn't make your relationship spiral to new heights or bond you for life as we often see in the movies. The irony of Hollywood is that although these actors and actresses portray this unrealistic idea, they experience personal failure in their own relationships. The bottom line is that sex and love are different animals. If sex were the same thing as love, Hollywood would be the happiest place on earth, and all film star marriages would be blissful. But you and I know this is not the case.

Don't confuse real life sex with the phony staged sex you see in the movies—and that goes for porn too! And don't sit there and pretend you never look either because I know better. I also know no bus load of cheerleaders is ever going to show up at your house and beg to get in your hot tub. For that matter, if your pool boy showed up wearing a sequined thong, you'd freak out, lock the door, and call 911. So get real and keep your mind in the game.

Sex does not mean there is love involved. Some people just have sex because it brings them pleasure or attention—or both. Others do it because they are bored, need money, love orgasms, want attention, crave acceptance, or are drunk. Make sure you know the difference! Do not confuse someone you love to have sex with (meaning you love the sex action) with someone you love.

Sex is undoubtedly one of the important factors in a fulfilling life. Yet, the power of sex has been much misunderstood and ultimately misused. The media tends to lead people astray, making them expect that every time will be perfect. In the movies or on television, there are no wet spots or accidental farts. This false image does not fit into the reality of the lives of millions of people worldwide who need both sex and love.

As the sex gets more frequent and graphic, we get bored; depictions of sex are now so pervasive, have so drenched the landscape, they are becoming nothing more than white noise. Who wants average sex after watching two beautiful actors banging for all their worth?

The Balls Are in Your Court

Marrying your money magnate is much the same as getting the car of your dream. Even if you score that Mercedes, you can't drive it off the lot, change the oil once, and expect it to run forever. In much the same way, you have to continually work at this relationship—especially after the ring is on your finger. So many people who seek to marry for money base their relationships around the ins and outs of the bedroom, which can be a big mistake. Let's face it: Sex is great but it can only go so far. Sex is a good way to captivate your millionaire momentarily—an eye-popping orgasm is a fabulous feeling. But that is all it is, a feeling, and a fleeting one at that. Millionaires, billionaires, and trillionaires get tired of the same old sex the same as the rest of us. It's like watching the same porn movie repeatedly; sure it turns you on initially, but after a while it becomes a bit repetitive.

Sex is extremely powerful because it changes the dynamics of your relationship permanently. And once you do the Humpty Dance, you've given away some of your power to attract. Once they've had their hand in nookie jar, they'll assume they can go back any time they want.

Also, keep in mind that some folks are just out for a quickie, and they change partners as often as they change underwear. I know it's hard to say no; I've been in those situations myself. But this is vital to your success. If your crotch is smoking like a '72 Ford with an oil leak, take the necessary precautions and don't put yourself in situations where you'll be tempted to give in to your hormones. Don't be alone with the other person, or take care of business before the date so you aren't hot to trot.

Sex can go two ways (and no I'm not referring to the front and back door). If the sex is bad, then you've just ruined your chances for marriage. If the sex is good, on the other hand, he or she is going to wonder why all of a sudden after a night of extreme pleasure you don't want to have another round. Not only does this build up some serious resentment, it also puts you in an awkward position of trying to explain yourself. Leave him or her breathless, begging for more, showing just enough to make them toss one off in the shower or reach for the vibrator. Dole out your sex as if were medicine in an eyedropper. Little by little. They have to want you so bad they can taste it.

Don't kiss when you are expected. Of course you want to, but keep things on your terms. Teach him or her the value of self discipline and that good things really do come to those who wait. The patience and self-control you practice will make you more desirable than anyone he or she has ever known. Yes, he or she can have you, but it has to be on your terms. Increase your perceived value in their minds.

This does not mean you should manipulate anyone or use sex as a weapon. In fact, this is an all too often truth to all those who married for "love." They use sex as a weapon to give them leverage. Never underestimate your position in the relationship or make any assumptions or expect that Goldilocks (or the Big Bad Wolf) should think, feel, or act the way you do. The main challenge you're going to find is the differences between the two of you.

My mother always told me never to marry anyone with the intention to change you. What you see is what you get. Well, with the exception of the late-night handcuffs and blindfolds, sexual desires and fetishes aren't exactly something a person advertises, especially if he or she is rich. But still, no PR campaign in the world can revive the image of a millionaire who got caught wearing a skintight latex suit while chained to the wall in the wine cellar.

Nice and Easy, Not Quick and Sleazy

Cultivating a successful relationship with your mogul is no different than one with the average Joe or Jane. But you have to keep him or her interested. There is nothing more detrimental to any relationship than falling into the same old routine day after day. After a while sex becomes monotonous too. A relationship should be based on good communication skills, trust, and interests. There's something to be said for romance and keeping the spark ignited. Bear in mind that people with money have the world at their fingertips, so if you don't keep them interested, they'll find something—or worse, someone—who will.

Take your time. Remember the phrase, "Why buy the milk if you can get the cow for free"? There is something to being said for not being easy. Rich people love exclusivity. So use this to your advantage. There are tons of men and women who are more than willing to give it up for money. Don't become just another notch on the dashboard of their Porsche. Give them just enough to want more.

Befriending and understanding your financial future is important, and as we've discussed previously, there are basically two types of people with money: bluebloods and self-mades. Bluebloods can be the most ridiculous and hard to deal with. You have to understand that when people are born with a golden spoon in their mouth, they love to be loved, adore being adored, and need to be needed. This can take a lot of time and energy, but by stroking their narcissistic tendencies, it will move you closer to them and you'll get to know what they're into, what they like and dislike, and what their style is. These types are usually into pleasure and spending all that cash some distant relative earned. They can also be extremely snooty and much less tolerant of imperfection.

The other group is the self-mades. The vast majority of the people on the Forbes 400 list earned their money themselves. Not only are these people more tolerant of less than perfect pedigrees, they are also easier to meet and get in touch with. They move in business circles, which allows you much more access than super-exclusive country clubs. Although they are passionate about business, which could result in a dinner or two alone, they are much less focused on looks and the material symbols of wealth. They don't generally know or care who wears designer what; they just make money, which is good for your long-term security.

A good tip when you are evaluating the possible whales in your part of the world is to think about the type of person you are and what kind of person you typically date. If you go for the high-maintenance type and don't mind the hassle of dealing with a PITA (pain in the ass), than a blueblood might suit. But if you'd rather jab your eye with an ice pick than date a guy who spends more than five minutes on his hair, the business type is probably your best option. Just don't expect a great deal of romance.

Successful marriages to money are built on friendship, just as they are in marriages for love. A shoulder to lean on and a good friend they can turn to is all anyone wants, the wealthy included. As I mentioned earlier, every material possession they desire is within their grasp; the only thing money can't buy is genuine companionship. This is your chance to step in and fulfill that need. It is really nothing more than supply and demand. They need something you're willing to give.

Don't hesitate to be helpful and supportive. Be the friend who rekindles that sparkle in her eye or puts a smile on his face. Be a trusted sounding board as you would in any other situation and create a real relationship based on sharing. This above all other things will make you vital in their life because you bring out their best in terms of personality and character. In you, they'll have found that friend to whom they can open up. Don't forget to always be there to celebrate the good times and to lend an ear whenever needed. Also remember that there are few things more therapeutic than a good laugh, so share your sense of humor.

Make him or her feel special, and letting this person know how he or she has touched your life in a unique way like no one else could. Be appreciative of his or her company and for making you smile. There is a certain amount of ego in wealthy people—or they wouldn't have amassed such amazing wealth. Make time each day to stroke that ego, and share their dreams, their world, and every aspect of their life. Always dream with them, build with them, and encourage and support them. Let them know they're your first thing in the morning and the last thing when you go to bed at night. Knowing their importance in your life and how much you enjoy their company will get you a convertible and dinner at Sardi's faster than any one-night stand ever would. Remember you want to own the bed you screw in, not just rent it by the hour.

Boobs, wax, hair, teeth, folds, wrinkles, and BOTOX are but the wrapping paper, the packaging. But nothing rivals the importance of communication when it comes to keeping your sugar-hun interested, sparked, sweet, and tweaked. The key to genuine companionship is communication, and 75 percent of communication is in active listening. That means you've got to shut up; it's not about you it's about your rich honey. Don't play "pretend interested" or you will be caught like a phony; you've got to be present and authentic. Master this skill, and you will be far ahead of anyone.

Novice salespeople, much like amateur money-chasers, get it wrong all the time. They talk too much. I let my sales people speak for 20 percent of the time they are in front of a prospect; the other 80 percent of the time should be spent listening. They gain so much more power when they understand the client—and so will you.

There is no better proof of genuine companionship than to be heard; it's the most elegant form of tacit flattery. This skill alone will let you in the circle even if all other prerequisites don't meet par.

"More than kinky, more than sex, your ability to listen will mean the difference between living rich or being the ex."

The Awkward Moment

There will be times you run across something just a bit out of the ordinary. You may want to plan for this eventuality and decide how you will handle an awkward moment in the boudoir. Just think of all the losers and crazy people you've dated. It's no different with the rich—although they don't simply buy a whip and pair of hip boots. They build a dungeon, hire a dominatrix, and film it live! Even those who seem pretty normal may make the odd request on occasion.

You want to define your own boundaries, sexual or otherwise, before you are in the situation. This is because by the time they bring up the kinky, you're already knee deep in nookie so it's more difficult to refuse if you want to do so. If you have a little of the dominatrix in you, however, then go for it but just be sure you can keep it up. I know it's fun to have a little fantasy now and then—I've even been known to don a pair of chaps, hat, and nothing else—but you don't necessarily want a rodeo every night.

It's worth saying that you will also run across other oddities—guys with a bent "member," women whose Wonderbras are truly wonders, and all sorts of other normal but strange presentations. Wealthy people are no different physically than the general population, and they also have the same insecurities about their bodies and sexual performance. You may be dating a billionaire who refuses to swim because he believes his legs are too skinny. You may run across an heiress who goes to great lengths to hide a birthmark she feels is too noticeable.

Having an imperfection sprung on you in the bedroom can be a little disconcerting. But how you handle it is vital. For example, one gold-digger I know, we'll call her Laci, discovered that her millionaire lover was uncomfortable donning a condom in her presence. Every time he needed to sheath the sword, he stole away to the walk-in closet, only to reappear, fists on hips, as "Condom Man"! If only he'd had a cape. Although Laci thought this act absolutely hilarious, she kept her composure and made him as comfortable as possible, and eventually this behavior stopped.

Joel is another example of having an odd habit sprung on him at an inopportune moment. Joel is dating an heiress who informed him of the "rules" for the bedroom. She will only have sex in the guest bedroom (one of seventeen she has) and then can't sleep unless she has her favorite tattered blanket. Joel made a game of surprising her in various bedrooms while always making sure he had her blankie close at hand. I have to wonder if she sucked her thumb as well, but Joel was willing to endure the strange requests of his PITA heiress.

All that said, don't be afraid to say no if you want to. People in this strata aren't very familiar with that word and hearing it on occasion is good for them—and makes you more attractive.

The Fox and the Heir

The best part of the start of a sexual relationship is, of course, the excitement. But sadly, some of the most exciting wealthy people are also married. This brings up a very important point. When you've been seeing someone and he or she is overly anxious to get you in the sack, don't assume it's your fabulous charm. "Trust but verify," as the Donald says. If they are sketchy about work or personal details, ask you not to meet them certain places, or call you only certain times of the day, then it should raise some red flags.

There are numerous people, wealthy or not, who constantly play the field. They troll online dating sites and chat rooms, hit on every member of the opposite sex, and take what they can get. The ultimate prize for these individuals is to convince you they are "almost" divorced so you still give them what they want while hoping they will leave their spouse. That is if you find out about the spouse at all.

One of the main characters from *Sex and in the City*, Carrie, was involved for years with Big, a married man. Eventually she got her man, but my view is that she just created a job vacancy! If Big cheated on his wife for years and then finally divorced her, what makes Carrie think it won't happen to her? You should write these words on you brain and never forget them: *Once a cheater, always a cheater.* If you pull your wealthy target out of a relationship, then, duh, someone else can do the same.

I want to point out that this is not just about men. Many married women who have no intention of divorcing like to have little flings on the side for a thrill. And it's nothing more than that—a thrill. You don't want to be one of those flings, so take some time and get to know your potential mate.

This brings up another "don't" when dealing with the wealthy. Don't do the help! If you try to get close to your target by sleeping with the chauffeur, maid, or bodyguard, not only will you prove that you will do anyone, but you also prove that you are beneath your wealthy target. Money does money, not the help! If you have a relationship with someone in his or her circle of friends, that's one thing. But anyone on the payroll is *off limits.*

Trust is a big factor within moneyed circles, and fraternizing with the worker bees raises concerns that the wealthy's most hidden secrets are being told to others. Once the word gets out that you've taken this road—and it will—you also lose all the valuable contacts who know your mogul. This can be devastating—especially if you've worked for months to get yourself into the right circles as it ruins your reputation for being one of them.

A wealthy mogul can easily choose to have a relationship with employees they spend a lot of time with, such as executive assistants. But they won't have relationships with others in that employee's circle of friends. It's one of those strange truths about human behavior.

You also must remember that wealthy people talk just like your circle of friends talk. If Mildred tells her girlfriends that the pool boy is easy, they all might give him a whirl, but that doesn't mean he'll walk away richer. You have to target a relationship/friendship first or you will just be an "also had." You will also never ascend into their accepted circle, which is vital. Sex gives you leverage, and sex can take it away—if you don't use it carefully.

It is a mistake to start banging away on the first date as it then becomes easy to view you as fulfilling just one need. This dissects the relationship and makes it very difficult for them to see you as marriage material. If they have no emotional attachment to you yet, it may never happen as you've given them the power. People often wonder how a man can keep a mistress and wife. The answer is that they fulfill different needs so he can compartmentalize them into separate areas of his life. Women tend to have a harder time not becoming emotionally involved once sex enters the picture, but that doesn't mean the guy will see things the same way.

I've encountered a bit of resistance to the idea of keeping sex and emotions separate (mostly from women), but it is completely necessary. You wouldn't walk into a corporate boardroom and burst into tears because your needs weren't being fulfilled. (At least I hope you wouldn't.) Once sex enters the arena, it clouds everyone's viewpoint. It's not that I'm recommending to abstain (That's just crazy talk!), but I am saying to view it for what it is and don't let you emotions blow this gig. You have to still be fun and undemanding and someone your honey wants to *be* with; not someone he or she has to *deal* with.

It's not unusual for wealthy individuals to have a hot night in the sack and then not call for three or four days. Not only are they probably unsure what to say, they are seeing how you will react. If your head starts to spin around and you become clingy, bet money they will dump your butt. But if you go on about your life with a great attitude like nothing happened, then it puts them in the position of wondering if you noticed. The chase is on! Be elusive; the fact that it is not at their discretion makes you all the more attractive. When people have to work for something, they appreciate it more.

The bottom line is that sex inevitably complicates things. If you feel secure that things are off to a good start, then by all means go for it and use the results to your advantage. The idea is to have your future benefactor at your heels, completely besotted. But you must travel this road carefully to maximize the benefits—including jewelry, furs, cars, and exotic vacations.

Sex can be dangerous territory but can also produce little heirs to the fortune. Whether you have an "accidental" pregnancy or are an unintentional sperm donor, the results can work in your favor. Even if you seriously do everything in the world not to procreate, if you engage in sex you know the risk. Who hasn't bought a pregnancy test now and again just to be sure the rabbit didn't die? Here again, it's a sword that cuts both ways. It can lead to something wonderful or be a complete disaster, depending on your particular money-honey.

Getting Dumped

There will be occasions, especially as you are starting out on the path to marry for money, where you blow it. You hop in the sack too fast or become overly obsessed. The next thing you know you get dumped. Don't worry; it happens, and the wealthy can be jerks. They may have the secretary call and dump you, or send a fax or text, and generally make you feel lower than a snail's slime trail. But now is not the time to despair!

Pick yourself up and stay visible, and soon you'll be back on the right path to riches once again. Keep the contacts you made while dating your former millionaire; there may even be one longing to comfort you through this difficult time. The worst thing you can do is disappear or take yourself out of circulation. The best thing you can do is snag one of his best friends so he has to be best man at the wedding!

Winning in this game is about understanding what to do and when, and even if you blow it, there is still hope to turn your experience into the lifestyle of your dreams. Most of all, realize that you are living the life. You got dumped by a millionaire—that's an accomplishment! The heart and mostly the ego will hurt for some time and you should stay true to your emotions, but never lose sight of your destination. Get back up, move on.

Summary

- ☾ Sex is key to a good marriage—even if you marry for money.
- ☾ Marriage looks different for all people.
- ☾ If sex and love were one and the same, Hollywood would be the happiest place on earth.
- ☾ Sex changes the dynamic of the relationship.
- ☾ Success in marriage is built on trust.
- ☾ Conversation is a skill that must be mastered.
- ☾ You can go kinky or not; it's up to you.

Ode to Lost Love

I met him at a party. There he was at the end of the buffet—
a loner, the last one on the plate. He had a certain something—
a sweetness, a sensuality. He was one hot cookie.
I felt as if I'd always known him, always hungered for him. When
he
looked at me with those warm brown eyes, I melted.
Before I knew it,
I had my hands on him, my mouth on him—in public.
After that night, we were inseparable.
With him, I could be myself. He didn't seem to care what mood I
was in, how I looked, even if I gained weight.
Together, we had the recipe for happiness.
No one satisfied me more than chip.
Then things changed. My friends said he was no good for me.
He started to give me heartburn.
I felt crummy, but it had no end.
Now we've gone our separate ways.
I hardly think of him anymore.
Oh, when I see a certain TV commercial,
a particular magazine ad,
a coupon for ten cents off—that old longing returns.
And when we run into each other in the supermarket,
we nod. We're friendly. But it's over.
—*Anonymous*

Seven: Prenups—Not Just for Schmucks!

I'm a great housekeeper. I get divorced. I keep the house.
—*Zsa Zsa Gabor*

"HOW COULD YOU?" "YOU DON'T understand." "If you really love me you will...." "If you really love me you won't...." Greedy, selfish, bitter, paranoid, sneaky. Like dollars from the ATM machine, so are the days of our prenups. The mere mention of this dastardly document transforms dainty ladies into foul-mouthed women who mysteriously regain their southern Louisiana accents, and makes even the toughest man curl up on the floor in a fetal position. Calm conversations soon become heated screaming matches. The prenuptial agreement provokes fear, distrust, and anger in most.

Prenups date back the 1700s and are becoming more and more popular each day. They were used traditionally by parties marrying for a second time and wanting to protect the property rights of children from an earlier marriage. They have also long been used when one party comes into the marriage with a business or significant inheritance. But as the rate of divorce has risen and many people are getting married later and with more assets, the practice of defining who gets what in the case of divorce has become more widely accepted.

For those of you who've been living on Mars or holed up in a trailer park your entire life watching daytime soaps, a prenuptial agreement is a signed and notarized agreement made by you and your millionaire before the wedding. This document covers various financial issues such as the control and possession of property (blah blah blah) and other assets taken into the marriage and later obtained during the marriage either individually or jointly, as well as the couple's future earnings (hearing test pattern), and how such property or assets will be distributed in the (legal mumbo jumbo) event of divorce or death. In layman's terms, once you sign this little legal jewel, you may not get squat. And just in case your honey's lawyer tries to pull a fast one, these agreements are also known as ante nuptial or premarital agreements.

Eighteenth-century shopkeeper Elizabeth Murray realized the value of a prenup. Obviously a woman ahead of her time, she insisted that her second and third husbands agree to pren-ups, which guaranteed her rights over certain personal property and her late husband's assets (denied most women in that era). Interestingly, by 2020, it is estimated that more than half of all marriages will have such an agreement as more and more women are climbing the financial ladder of success.

Just as the divorce rate of modern marriages has risen to nearly 50 percent, the "just in case" practice of signing pre-nuptial contracts has also grown. The days of moonlight and romance are over. We live in an age of contracts and legality. Today, law firms estimate that about 10 percent of first mar-riages and 20 percent of second marriages now have a prenup attached. And with good reason. Statistics show that one in three of all first marriages end up in a divorce while half of second or third ones crumble. These are scary numbers to those who have spent their lives amassing a fortune. The wealthy aren't willing to watch all that work walk out the door because of a bad decision.

Before we go any further, I need to give you my disclaimer. Just because I'm writing a chapter on prenups does not make me qualified to give any legal advice. I'm only qualified to make you laugh and maybe find a millionaire to spend the rest of your life with. So I plead, beg, urge, or otherwise motivate you to obtain legal counsel before considering any matter pertaining to contracts or any other legal documents.

There are attorneys who specialize in prenups and who can give you an idea of what to expect. Odds are you will probably meet some of them at those fancy benefits and art gallery openings you'll be attending as they work hard to schmooze their rich clients. Again, party chatter can be your friend as you ask about the oddest prenup requirements they've ever encountered. Although this is likely to be a humorous exchange, it can quickly move to what the average prenup might look like for people like your money-honey. Free legal advice over martinis is always a great thing.

More than likely, before you take a stroll down the aisle, your mogul will ask you to sign a prenuptial agreement. If he or she doesn't, I'd be suspicious and a bit leery, frankly. I mean, if they're not smart enough to ask for a prenup, then they may not be smart enough to hold onto their money long enough for you to enjoy it.

In many instances of families with massive amounts of money, children are not only born with a silver spoon in the mouth, they're also holding a prenup in their little fingers. Daddy and Mommy Snobbolats would be absolutely horrified if Junior squandered the family fortune on the town tramp. Your first reaction when asked to sign one of these legal chastity belts will more than likely be "#@%& no!" Granted, signing a prenup may make you feel like a second-class citizen or a money-grubbing fiend, but if you want to live the lifestyle of the rich and fabulous, you're going to have to make certain accommodations. If you don't sign, then it's entirely possible your dreamboat won't marry you—and you'll be back schlepping shoes or selling perfume at Dillard's. Worse still, you've already become accustomed to this way of living and now the red carpet could be yanked out from beneath your feet.

To me, a prenup is no different than insurance for your car or home. Just because you purchase a policy doesn't mean you're going to drive off a cliff or burn your house down. But if you do, you're covered. Who knows? The world could end tomorrow, but has this stopped you from living your life? Remember, your fiscal fiancé knows that without this important prenuptial agreement he is potentially jeopardizing his entire financial future.

Wealthy people made their money by taking emotions out of life situations and replacing them with contracts and legalese, and marriage is no exception. Sure, they want to be loved, but they also want to cover their asses. Marriage to them is a business partnership with benefits. They want to protect this emotional, physical, and financial union to the best of their abilities. So sign it with a smile. Work things out now while the petals of the roses have not yet wilted rather than tomorrow after months or years of bitter name-calling. It guarantees you the lifestyle you want. Stop worrying about the what-if's.

Before the Petals Wilt

What most people don't realize is that in every marriage there's a hidden contract. That's right; with every marriage license there is a secret decoder prenup. When you sign your marriage license, you think you're agreeing to the same lifestyles and goals as your spouse, but like millions of couples before you, it won't be long before you discover you were mistaken. Would you ever sign a contract for a house, business, or loan sight unseen? Of course not. You want to know certain factors, such as interest rate and payment terms.

Each of us entered into our marriage (which is a legal contract) with the assumption that our spouse knows the ground rules and boundaries as we understand them. Before your marriage, you may have discussed some items—who does the dishes, pays the bills, or takes out the trash. But I'm willing to bet that neither of you wrote any of these expectations down.

Three kids, a mortgage, two car payments, and 20 pounds later, you two are bitching at each other nonstop. "It's your turn." "No, I asked you to do it." "How come you never help me anymore?" Those cute little conversations between each kiss on the couch about how much you love each other and how you're going to do everything as a team are long forgotten.

The expectations in those initial chats, or as I like to call them "nonverbal marriage contracts," apply to every aspect of your life including:

(Family
(Friends
(Power
(Sex
(Money
(Children

These are all-encompassing and important matters. Sure, he may not mind that you go for a pedicure with your mother every weekend now. She may have no problem with your annual pilgrimage to your alma mater's homecoming game with your fraternity buddies. In the beginning. But wait. Sometime after the first few months of marriage, if not sooner, a broken contract clause will pop up like a jack-in-the-box on crack.

The most amazing part is that it happens over the most trivial of matters. It may begin when you expect her to fix you a sandwich for your lunch or he wants you to cover him with a blanket when he's sick. You may have watched your parents do this for each other and automatically expected it to be done for you. Your partner, on the other hand, may hate sandwiches and never gets sick. If he or she doesn't know or understand the conditions you thought were agreed upon during one of your late night cuddle sessions, you're likely to feel angry, hurt, betrayed, confused, and SOL. In the beginning, you kiss and make up, forgiving each minor infraction, but as months and years pass, the pieces of the broken contract will pile up and eventually your marriage may be in trouble—all because of this invisible marriage contract. What you assumed was understood, what they assumed would be understood, was not. I've always said that the most common mistake in communication is the presumption that it has been achieved.

Your assumptions are unconscious or only vaguely understood by you. You only truly become aware of them when your husband or wife makes you so mad you want to douse their clothes with gasoline in the front yard and light a match. Every time you or your partner don't live up to these invisible contracts, you become more resentful.

A prenup lays the ground rules for what you can expect from the marriage in case you separate. It's best to do it while you are civil not livid. A prenup is also an unconventional way to learn more about your spouse. All expectations in the marriage are verbalized and written down, and some of these may surprise you. For example, you may assume that if you have children, she will stay home when they are sick. She, on the other hand, may want you to do it or split the duty equally. With a prenup, there will be fewer disagreements later on in the marriage. But if it happens, just glide up your spiral staircase, spin the dial, and take the document out of the safe. A prenup ensures both you and your partner both clearly understand the full ramifications of what you are really saying. While most prenups focus on division of property, many have conduct clauses and other strange items.

Every Cloud Has a Golden Lining

You're checking the guest list for one last time and confirming your honeymoon reservations, and out of the blue a prenup is shoved in front of you. Don't be insulted; instead take the time to evaluate the situation. I know these agreements may seem insincere, but often they protect you as well. So many times, I hear people complain that a prenup is nothing more than a cruel form of manipulation. If your fiancée were a maniacal control freak, you'd find out long before the engagement. You're not marrying Attila the Hun, so this should not be a problem. A prenup helps to ensure the financial well-being of the marriage, nothing more. What most people don't realize is that the prenup can be crafted to be advantageous to you. You may not feel as though you have a choice in this manner, but you really do. If used properly, it gives you a chance to negotiate, and whatever you achieve gets down on paper. Believe it or not, having this prenup discussion might actually help build a mutual trust and relieve anxiety about getting married.

Stop for a moment and try to consider the other person's feelings. Maybe he or she doesn't even want to ask you but is feeling pressured by family or an attorney. Don't make a big stink and storm out the door in a tiff. This type of behavior only gives ammunition to family and friends who don't like you in the first place. "Well, if so-and-so is acting that way now, imagine how unbearable she'll be five years from now."

> Even if you can convince your millionaire to marry you without a prenup, you're still not as safe as you would be with one.

Even if you can convince your millionaire to marry you without a prenup, you're still not as safe as you would be with one. Fast forward ten years; your spouse dies in a car accident. Don't start singing and dancing over the windfall yet. The family who hated you then more than likely never really grew to love you. Have you ever heard of a contested will? If your wealthy spouse's family is looked on more favorably by the court than you are, they don't have to be generous or guarantee you security. They are not obligated to treat you as your spouse would if he were alive.

The fact that you are reading this book is a strong indicator you're not the financial heavyweight in the relationship, so let's look at a few ways this prenup can put you in a better financial position. This is a fine opportunity to negotiate your position in the marriage. If you argue and refuse to sign only to relent later, you've limited yourself to what the other person wants. But, by being agreeable, you may be able to include a clause stating, for instance, that if your spouse commits adultery, you get a certain amount of money. Prenups are fabulous opportunities for you to carve out a little nest egg for yourself. When both of you are happy and eagerly anticipating the big day, you're in a much stronger position for generosity than you would be standing in a court room glaring at each other. Always, without fail, position yourself to get more than the law would allow without a prenup.

With a prenup, you're able to clarify expectations and rights for your future. This gives you a sense of security in case of death or divorce. If you still insist on no way, no how, never in a million years, no prenup, then the least you can do is to protect yourself by learning about your state's laws specific to marriage and find out if there is any protection. Most states are equitable distribution states where the laws of the state will consider what each partner contributed financially to the marriage and if divorce occurs, assets are divided according to your contribution. It may be approximately a 50-50 split but not necessarily. For the most part, assets or inheritances brought into the marriage are not considered joint assets. But the day you get married, the clock starts ticking. So if you marry a wealthy person who doesn't work or can't work for any reason, there may not be much of a contribution to your personal account, if any. In the final scene, you could be shut out. With nothing.

When you get married without a prenup, you are voluntarily agreeing to the laws of the state in which you live. If you've ever stood in a line to renew your driver's license or called a state agency for any reason, you know exactly the kind of brain power I'm talking about. Why in the world would you trust your future to these people? Besides, no one but you has your best interest in mind. When you have a prenup, you and your millionaire have decided what you want and it is likely to be very different from what state law may or may not give you. If death or divorce comes, you may not be happy, but at least you will be protected with a prenup.

Openness and honest communication is invaluable for

fairly negotiating your prenup. Just because you don't have the financial stronghold in the relationship, doesn't mean you have no power. If you handle yourself and your emotions correctly, greed won't enter the picture. Both of you have needs, and this agreement can be something with which you can both live happily. A successful prenup is when you get what you need, although it may seem that you aren't getting what you want.

Which Prenup Is Best for You?

There are differences and variations in prenups as there are in people. Everyone has to customize their agreement to meet their specific needs. You must respect each other above all to work out the best possible prenuptial agreement.

First, let's look at some of the more interesting requests and huge blunders made by people who should have known better:

(Roseanne Barr fired her attorney in 1990 for bringing up the idea that she should sign a prenup before saying "I do" to Tom Arnold. Four years later the couple divorced, and I bet Tom grinned all the way to the bank with his 50 million bucks.

(Catherine Zeta-Jones and Michael Douglas have what is known as an escalation clause. Many prenups where an older rich person marries a younger person contain these. An escalation clause basically states that for each year the marriage endures, the young spouse receives additional compensation. In Zeta-Jones's case, that's an additional 2.8 million dollars per year.

(A not-so-smart move is to have a sunset clause rather than an escalation clause. A sunset clause sets a definite date for the provisions of the prenuptial agreement to end. This sounds like a nice reward of trust and commitment for a long-term marriage—but it doesn't always work out that way. Jack Welch put this sort of provision into his prenup with wife Jane Beasley Welch. The problem is, the second that date passed, Jane was free to go—which she did, taking an estimated 150 million dollars of Jack's hard-earned money with her.

☾ As unbelievable as it may sound, items such as who gets the pets, the maid, the pool boy, and the groundskeepers are sometimes specified in prenups. Although it may seem degrading to lump household staff in with the pets, its actually elevating them to members of the family, and everyone who is anyone knows how hard it is to find good help.

☾ Even things such as cheating can include a monetary compensation should it occur. Now I ask you, who marries someone expecting they will cheat? Cheaters, that's who! A famous example of this is Charlie Sheen and Denise Richards, whose prenup stated that if either of them cheated, the other spouse got an additional 4 million dollars in an ensuing divorce (which did happen!). Makes you wonder why they got married at all, doesn't it?

☾ Another area that is sometimes put into prenups are drug and alcohol use provisions. In Nicole Kidman and Keith Urban's prenup, there is a provision that pays him an additional 640,000 dollars for each year Keith abstains from using illegal drugs. If he fails, he doesn't get squat from her estimated 150-million-dollar fortune. Talk about scared straight!

There are an untold number of provisions you can add to a prenup. Things like no poker nights with the buddies and no going on vacation with the mother-in-law. There have also been weight requirements and exercise schedules included.

Generally, most of the provisions will concern protecting the long-term assets. Through a combination of negotiating escalation clauses and sunset provisions, you have the opportunity to improve your position. Remember, this is not about what you are worth; it's about what you can negotiate. So be creative.

Leveraging the Prenup

The emotional aspects of being presented with a lengthy prenup must be anticipated and dealt with in advance. Much like controlling your emotions in the bedroom when presented with something unexpected, you must also control your emotions and react positively no matter how you may be feeling at the time. You have to keep in mind that many prenups are tossed out by the court if it is found the prenup doesn't suit the current circumstances. And circumstances change all the time. Even if your millionaire puts in odd provisions like who gets the chef, it can actually work in your favor.

In court, judges uses common sense and reason. When they are presented a prenup in a divorce case and that prenup has provisions such as weight limits, who gets the gardener, and other ridiculous provisions, they may (and frequently do) conclude that the prenup was not really a good faith protection of assets and was an emotional proposition instead. You have to remember that the whole idea of the prenup is asset protection not behavior control, so when your intended inserts clauses and provisions that smack of behavior control, it can be considered a misuse of the intended purpose of a prenup and backfire. This works to your advantage. So when you see silly requirements in a legal document, go with it, and if it's ever brought up as a reason for divorce you may have a great chance to get a fabulous settlement.

In addition, many spouses claim duress at the time of signing the prenup because it is frequently done shortly before the wedding. This is an emotional time and the courts know it, so you can use that argument to great advantage.

Be sure to get your own legal advice before signing. An attorney can negotiate longevity provisions and escalation clauses that reward you for staying married, and judges view these as good because their basic premise is that you will not divorce. So if it comes down to a divorce at some point, it shows that your intention in the prenup was to stay married—not to take the money and run.

Although we'd all like to think that legal determinations are unbiased and fair, the truth is that the people who present themselves in the best light are viewed more favorably in the eyes of the judge. This is one reason you often see the details of an affair dragged into divorce court. The why of a divorce isn't materially applicable to division of property, but it does determine how the judge views that person. You want to be the good guy, so be careful how you conduct yourself if it looks like the marriage might be heading for a breakup.

Although it may seem a little premature to talk about all these instances before you even snag Mr. or Ms. Money Bags, it is important to anticipate a prenup and logically think through any surprises that might be on it and how you will handle them. This gives you leverage. The mere act of presenting a prenup can be stressful for your intended as well, so your positive reaction can give him or her a great deal of comfort—and feeling of generosity as you start your new life together.

The Prenup Grudge

One of the worst things you can do is to hold onto a grudge because your money-honey insisted you sign a prenup. A grudge is pent-up anger that is held onto way after the situation has passed and can become passive-aggressive behavior if you allow it to fester. You must sign the prenup and let it go—just get over it and put it out of your mind. This means you don't mention it every time an opportunity presents itself, as in: "Why don't you buy the house in Tahoe? It's not like you have anything to lose; you have the prenup." It also means that you don't repeat it constantly in front of friends to embarrass your spouse; in fact, you should never mention it at all to anyone. If you continue to allow it to fester, your new spouse can become your ex in a heartbeat—and damn glad you did sign that prenup.

I have seen newlyweds carry a grudge for one reason or another through the wedding and into the marriage, and it's a disaster no matter what the circumstances. When you go around feeling like a victim you attract negative events. You also run off the one thing you have been after this whole time—a rich spouse. Not only is the prenup an issue, but just getting past the wedding and into married bliss can be difficult. Smart gold-diggers keep a cool head at all times and do whatever is needed to ensure the festivities go off without a hitch. You want your new spouse full of positive and wonderful memories, not focused on your telling off her mother at the reception.

Small irritations in transitioning from dating to marrying a millionaire can accumulate just under the surface like a low-grade infection, taking away your chance to enjoy the good life. They can also escalate insignificant issues into drawn-out battles. Once the lines are drawn, it's hard to get back to peace.

You Can't Fight City Hall

You have all heard the phrase "You can't fight city hall." To me that means you have to choose your battles wisely—especially in the early days of the marriage. If you are carried across the threshold and instantly demand that your mother move in and his kids get shipped to boarding school, you are on very uncertain ground. This is especially true if you come up against your new spouse's family. Her mother may see you as a bum and her kids may see you as a direct threat to their inheritance, so don't be fooled by their quasi-friendly demeanor. Ravines are full of undiscovered bodies of gold-diggers who stepped on too many toes.

Rich families have more at stake, so you should be prepared to navigate shark-infested waters. The last thing you want to do is to have them gang up on you and convince your new spouse he or she made a mistake. I suggest you look at the prospect of marriage to a wealthy person much like a game of "Survivor." You must figure out everyone's real thoughts and motivations, and create alliances that will assist you in making it as easy as possible to attain and retain your booty. And never forget that you are expendable. You must insinuate yourself into the fabric of the family and become the in-law everyone loves—not the one they love to hate. This will, of course, take a great deal of time and energy, but it does get easier over time as the family slowly accepts you.

You must resign yourself to the fact that there will probably be some family members who will always resent your intrusion into their lives. Perhaps they are still friends with your spouse's ex or they don't think you are a good match. The best course of action in these instances is to be a strong contributing member to family events so their disparaging remarks eventually are given no credence. You must not let them push you around or treat you like a second-class citizen. Even if you are concerned they could negatively impact you financially, you must not let these naysayers scare you or convince you to sit in the corner and take what they dish out. Stand your ground and bite back, if needed. Secretly they will eventually admire the fact that you had the balls to tell them to back off.

Tricks and Treats

Not only is the prenup used by many families to scare off and get rid of what they consider an "undesirable" element, if they suspect it's money you are after, they may also offer you a settlement to go away. There are two directions you can go here: You can take the money, but that means you sacrifice a great deal. You will be marked as undesirable for any of your prospect's friends or business partners. No one wants to be with the person who just got paid off to get out of town! All your hard work will have been for naught. So if you go this route, it better be enough money to make it worth your while.

The other direction it can go is for you to be offended and morally indignant—rejecting their offer and making it clear your intentions are honorable. This can also be a good bonding experience with your millionaire if he or she finds out, which, of course, you will make sure of. After all, how can anyone put a price on what you have together? This circumstance will set you up as the victim and set the millionaire against his or her own. This gives you the ultimate power to get the wedding on the way. Elope if the opportunity presents itself and get that ring on your finger.

To get into the marrying-for-money game and win, you must be willing to pull out all the tricks, treats, and wiles you possess—and even learn some new ones. Endurance and persistence in the face of challenges could mean the difference between you driving a Mercedes and enjoying massages every day, or flipping burgers on the weekend to make ends meet. So make the commitment to go all the way.

Summary

(Prenups provoke fear, anger, and distrust.

(A prenup is like insurance.

(Every marriage has a hidden contract.

(A prenup lays the groundwork for rules for the relationship.

(Let your emotions go and think like a business-person.

Eight: Wiping With Ben Franklins

> When you've got them by their wallets, their hearts and minds will follow.—*Fern Naito*

REMEMBER THE TV SHOW "LIFESTYLES OF the Rich and Famous"? We all imagine millionaires sipping expensive champagne at breakfast, driving luxury cars, shopping at the most exclusive stores, and traveling to the world's most exotic locations. Portraying the lifestyle of a millionaire spouse isn't easy. There are many standards of living that need to be addressed. To portray the millionaire lifestyle, you must make sure you you're comfortable with nothing but the absolute best, and there is no limit to whatever you want. Remember, wealth is just as much about your mindset as it is about your bank account.

You've spent the last year hobnobbing with the rich and fabulous. Christmas in Vail. Summer in Paris. Yes, you're somewhat accustomed to this lifestyle, but once the honeymoon is over, how different is your life going to be when you're the spouse rather than the lover? How different are you going to have to act? What exactly is expected of you? How is this new millionaire status going to affect you?

Adjusting to your new way of living takes a bit of getting used to, but once you do, your life will never be the same. Your life will be on display; all eyes will be on you at charity events, golf tournaments, and museum openings. You will be the source of gossip: "Did he marry her just for money?" "I can't believe she wore those shoes."

Not long ago, while I was waiting to get my hair cut, I overheard the manicurist talking to her client. These two women were dishing the dirt about a stylist in the salon who married an older man for his money. "I know she doesn't love him." "I hope it's worth it." The more these ladies dished the dirt, the more I realized it was because of jealousy. They had no genuine concern for their "friend." I was waiting for their heads to spin around and fly off their neck.

What really happens when you have enough money to buy almost anything in the world? To begin with, your days of shopping at Wal-Mart are over. Your list of essential items changes from wanting a comfortable home to deciding at which mansion, chalet, or villa to spend the summer. Let's take a look at just a few of the money-is-no-object must-haves.

> What really happens when you have enough money to buy almost anything in the world? To begin with, your days of shopping at Wal-Mart are over.

Staff. Butlers, maids, chaffers, chefs, and personal assistants are at your disposal to help make your life easy and relaxing. They eliminate tedious everyday activates such as answering the phone, scheduling appointments, driving, maintaining the household, and cooking. Keep in mind, your staff can't work twenty-four/seven, so you'll want to make certain you have back-up staff. Most millionaires and billionaires employ anywhere from two to three sets of staff because they usually have a traveling staff, and if they have children they need a set for them too.

And then, of course, there are the personal assistants. If you still can't believe all of this is true and haven't quite adjusted your mindset yet, you can have them reaffirm this by telling you how rich you are on a daily basis.

Estates. Notice I said "estates," not house, not mansions, and certainly not just one. Wealthy people take the potato chip approach to life. You can't have just one. Privacy and exclusivity are an added benefit. If you don't want someone on your property, they don't get through the security gates. Many keep second, third, or even fourth residences all over the world. One particular commonality is New York City, Bermuda, London, and Vail.

The estates of Oracle CEO Larry Ellison and Bill Gates are fabulous examples of unlimited budgets. Larry Ellison's lavish Woodside, California, estate is estimated to be worth 100 million dollars, and features feudal Japanese architecture, a manmade lake, and some seven outbuildings. Microsoft mogul Bill Gates relaxes in his 60-foot swimming pool complete with an underwater stereo. Built into a hillside on the edge of Lake Washington, his 66,000-square-foot home has a 1,000-square-foot dining room.

Another benefit—no mortgage payments, if you choose the nonleveraged variety of millionaire. Why bother with troublesome banks and worry about high interest rates when you can just write a check for 50 million dollars and be on your way?

Travel. While the rest of the families in America are suffering on cross-country trips in SUVs packed with screaming kids, a barking dog, too much luggage, and a mother sedated on Valium, you are floating through the streets in air-conditioned luxury in the backseat of your Bentley as your chauffeur navigates those pesky traffic snarls. As a matter of fact, you never have to drive again.

If driving is too tedious for you (I know it is for me), then why not fly? And I'm not talking about Continental or American. You never again have to sit like a contortionist in coach for hours on end. No more will you have to listen to smelly old ladies break wind in the seat next to you while the man on the other side snores and drools on his denim overalls. Say goodbye to crappy peanuts and stale cheese and peanut butter crackers passed off as in-flight meals. You, my rich friend, have your own personal jet. These planes, which can accommodate as many as sixteen passengers (don't forget the help; you don't want to have to unpack your own suitcase), usually sell for about 15 million dollars and up, depending on the make, mileage, and amenities. Your jet can have every amenity you can think of. Although they are shared, these chartered jets do not skimp on luxury. Flat-screen TVs, a master suite with a king-size bed, a marble shower, and comfortable plush leather recliners can be yours to enjoy.

Yachts. I'm not talking about Gilligan and the S.S. *Minnow,* I'm talking megayachts. Bill's buddy, Paul Allen of Microsoft, has a megayacht worth more than 200 million dollars with a permanent crew of sixty, two helicopters, a ten-man submarine, and seven boats. If a submarine makes you too claustrophobic, and you feel outnumbered by the staff you can downsize to a modest vessel, complete with a gym, home theater, and jet skis.

The Island Life. No more all-inclusive Mexico resorts ruined by obnoxious drunk spring breakers. Bermuda is the island of choice. Pink sand beaches and clear water are just part of the package; the best aspect of Bermuda is that the British culture of the island respects the privacy of its millionaire guests.

If the thought of sharing a beach with others is too much to bear, there is always the private island. This is an absolute must-escape destination to keep publicity at a minimum. The combination of luxury and seclusion makes this an ideal purchase. Whether renting or purchasing, private islands hold an unparalleled sense of seclusion. Media mogul, Ted Turner has two, one off the coast of South Carolina and one in Hawaii. Richard Branson made famous Necker Island, his own personal retreat in the British Virgin Islands.

Your Own Credit Card. Now I don't mean just any old Visa or MasterCard. The wealthy even have their own credit card. American Express' Centurion Card, aka the "Black AmEx," is available only by invitation. This card is designed for those customers who travel frequently, and who want and need high levels of personalized service. Since it is by invitation only, it's not a mainstream product and the Black Card is so exclusive that American Express will say very little about it or any of its privileges, rewards, or statistics.

Luxurious Amenities. Say goodbye to microwave popcorn, domestic beer, and handheld massagers. Gourmet kitchens, first-class spas, designer linens, and state-of-the-art electronics are just a few of the amenities you will enjoy on a daily basis. And you don't have to search for these wonderful items if you don't want to. Jewelers, high-end car makers, and numerous other vendors who cater to the wealthy will bring the selection to you. No muss, no fuss, and no long lines to stand in. No matter what your whim, someone will find it and bring it to you, and you never have to lift a finger.

Party Like It's 1999—Million Dollars

Millionaire parties are outrageously lavish. With glamorous birthday party favors and world-class entertainment, extravagant themed parties make ice cream and cake a thing of the past. The mega wealthy pride themselves on outdoing one another in more ways than just pricey invitations and outrageous entertainment when these turning point events roll around. Milestone birthdays call for the most extravagant blowout celebrations imaginable, sometimes costing well over six figures, taking place in international luxury resorts and including many celebrities and other A-list guests.

When Oprah Winfrey turned fifty, she sent birthday invitations to fifty of her closest female friends asking them to lunch at the Bel Air Hotel. Later, she hosted a dinner party at her Santa Barbara ranch and finally threw a star-studded birthday bash, which allegedly cost hundreds of thousands of dollars. John Travolta also celebrated his fiftieth birthday in typical costly style. His wife, Kelly Preston, sent birthday invitations to 280 of their closest friends. She hosted a surprise party for him in Cabo San Lucas, Mexico, at the Palmilla luxury resort.

The birthday party invitation list included many VIP guests.

Coming-of-age birthdays generally call for over-the-top celebrations. Paris Hilton's twenty-first birthday was celebrated at exotic locals all over the world and all in one day, allegedly costing 75,000 dollars each. While you were enjoying a progressive dinner around the trailer park, she shared birthday invitations for her exorbitant shindigs in Tokyo, London, Los Angeles, Las Vegas, and New York.

Bubba Don't Live Here

While the fabulous wonders of your new life can make your head spin, you must take it all in stride. You can't pull a Gomer Pile and proclaim "Gwaaahhhleee!" every time you come across some other amazing benefit of wealth. Remember I mentioned in a previous chapter that you can spot pretenders because of how obnoxious they become and how readily they flash their cash? This is what is known by bluebloods as "new money," or more appropriately, white trash with money. You must learn to incorporate a wealthy mindset or you will find yourself sliding back into your old ways—just with more cash. One of the problems is that the friends and family you from your former life with whom you may still associate may not have made the leap. They can quickly lull you back into the low-rent mindset. Following are a few things that might be an indication you are sliding a bit in convincing your new spouse you belong in that palatial mansion.

1. You ask for a flyswatter. Rich people don't swat flies. They have people for that. Call a maid, butler, chauffeur, or whoever, but don't swing that piece of plastic on a wire yourself.

2. Someone invites you to the nutcracker. You think this means you stand on the high dive for an hour wondering when they are going to show to see you display you skill by leaping into the deep end. Sometimes it pays to run such a request by someone—anyone—who might

have a better understanding. Of course, you will be a never-ending source of entertainment for the staff, who hope you crack those nuts permanently.

3. You look for the closet light in the chalet for twenty minutes only to discover that it's a switch not a string. Rich people's closets are vast chasms that could be more than 1,000 square feet in size. It is important to know what goes where so you don't end up with your lingerie in the sweater drawers. In this instance, you follow the lead of your new spouse or visit an organizer store with a photo of the space and ask the staff there. They don't know you, and you can tell them it's a friend's closet but you're not certain about what goes where. If you are lucky, they will be nice and tell you. If you're not so lucky, they will see the opportunity to mess with a newly rich person and convince you that those shoe cubbies are for extra tampons or for collecting bottles of beer.

4. There are these odd brown spots on the lawn of the estate. For men convenience is everything, but you're rich now. Don't take a leak on the lawn just because you don't want to walk up to the big house. Of course, if you have to take a dump behind a palm tree, you have a wallet full of Ben Franklin's for wiping.

5. Uncle Frank's Peterbilt sits in the circle drive underneath the portico and Cousin Eddie's RV sits out by the tennis court draining blue water into the koi pond. Treat your relatives right, but save them from themselves. Of course, they may just want to save you the "trouble" escorting them to the mansion in style, but you must make them believe it's no problem.

A Touch of Class

There are certain distinctions between trashy and classy, and you must know the difference to keep up your station in life. The idea of class has many facets, and it goes beyond your level of cash. Class can't be bought, and manners have become a rare commodity. When was the last time you watched an impudent heiress upbraid some poor worker on a reality show? That's not class.

Wealthy men and women tend to have impeccable manners, and they expect the same of you. This is a lifelong expectation and does not end when you say "I do." You must continue to exude charm and grace. This means you are not boastful nor do you yell at the help or make them miserable. Conduct yourself in all situations with style and grace, exuding a calm, peaceful existence—not a bitchy insistence. Just because you have money, there is no excuse to treat people poorly. Especially because poorly treated employees and associates can write tell-all books.

> Wealthy men and women tend to have impeccable manners, and they expect the same of you.

Nothing can make you new spouse run for the hills faster than being embarrassed by your poor behavior or bad manners. You will never regret taking the high road in any situation that is presented, and you will frequently be noted as one of those few nice rich people. Give your new other half reason to brag about you and all that you do.

Baby Makes Two

Of course any union can possibly produce offspring. Once you bring your baby home from the hospital, your life will change—but not in the ways you think. Most new parents suffer from sleep deprivation and live in constant fear of making mistakes. Not the wealthy; that's what nannies are for. There will always be someone there to handle the small hassles while you just enjoy your children. It is really every mother's dream to not have to worry about cleaning, cooking, and keeping everyone on track, and when you marry well, you get to reap all the rewards and great memories with none of the sleep deprivation and stress most parents face.

Once the kids get older, it only gets better; you can spoil them in ways unimaginable. When Tori Spelling was five, her father Aaron Spelling wanted her to have a white Christmas. Since they were living in California at the time, you would think this to be an impossible feat. Not for the mega rich! On Christmas Day a truck from Barrington Ice in Brentwood spread snow in the backyard and added a Styrofoam snowman. Five years later, Aaron hired a snow machine to blow out so much powder it created a sledding hill. It must have been amazing dressing in snowsuits and sledding down a snow-covered hill while it's 85 degrees outside. Only the mega rich can pull this off.

You may also experience an interesting shift in the attitude of your money-honey's family. Before you were a gold-digger, but now you are the mother to an heir or the chosen sperm donor of a new branch of the family tree. Once you produce spawn of a millionaire, you are forever connected to the family and their fortune, and they know it. Although you may end up with a divorce, you will never completely leave the family.

Your Dreams Are Within Your Grasp

It doesn't matter if you currently file endless piles of paperwork, schlep syrup at the Waffle House, or scrub toilets for a living. Even if you spend more time under the hood of a car than in front of the TV, you can marry well and live a life of luxury and ease if you focus on the prize and take the steps necessary to achieve it. In truth, it's not that hard to marry the wealthy because contrary to popular belief, they are people just like you and me.

Although this book is great fun, it also contains kernels of truth and wisdom about relationships. We are a very emotional species these days, and that's not always a good thing. Although society frowns on marrying for money, it seems to approve of the crapshoot technique of falling in love. If that really worked, we wouldn't be in these desperate times with few people maintaining any kind of long-term relationship. You may have been shocked, surprised, and intrigued by this book's content but in the end I would guess that you also see some truths.

Whether you close these pages and go out in the world to seek a money-honey for yourself or not, if any words or concepts that I've conveyed give you a new perspective on marriage and the reasoning behind our choices, then I will have accomplished my mission. There are no sure things, regardless of which path you choose. But by putting yourself out there, you give the possible a chance rather than settling for the probable. I wish you love, life, happiness—and of course, a happy hookup with your dream millionaire.

Summary
- (You have every reason to deserve to be happy.
- (Adjusting to your new lifestyle can be much more difficult than you think.
- (Financial arrangements and agreements can be approached with logic and reason when love isn't in the way.
- (Learning how to live rich forever can be accomplished but it takes practice.
- (The life you have always dreamed of is well within your grasp.